# Magic Crystals, Sacred Stones

The Magical Lore of Crystals
Minerals and Gemstones

# Magic Crystals, Sacred Stones

The Magical Lore of Crystals
Minerals and Gemstones

Mélusine Draco

AXIS MUNDI
BOOKS

Winchester, UK
Washington, USA

First published by Axis Mundi Books, 2012
Axis Mundi Books is an imprint of John Hunt Publishing Ltd., Laurel House, Station Approach,
Alresford, Hants, SO24 9JH, UK
office1@jhpbooks.net
www.johnhuntpublishing.com
www.axismundi-books.com

For distributor details and how to order please visit the 'Ordering' section on our website.

Text copyright: Mélusine Draco 2011

ISBN: 978 1 78099 137 5

A CIP catalogue record for this book is available from the British Library.

Design: Stuart Davies

Printed and bound by CPI Group (UK) Ltd, Croydon, CR0 4YY

We operate a distinctive and ethical publishing philosophy in all
areas of our business, from our global network of authors to
production and worldwide distribution.

# CONTENTS

**Chapter titles are taken from music composed by George Rochberg**

# Author Biography

Mélusine Draco originally trained in the magical arts of traditional British Old Craft with Bob and Mériém Clay-Egerton. She has been a magical and spiritual instructor for over 20 years with Arcanum and the Temple of Khem, and writer of numerous popular books on traditional witchcraft and ritual magic. Her highly individualistic teaching methods and writing draws on ancient sources, supported by academic texts and current archaeological findings.

Her *Traditional Witchcraft* series is published by Moon Books, an imprint of John Hunt Publishing: *Traditional Witchcraft for Urban Living, Traditional Witchcraft for the Seashore, Traditional Witchcraft for Fields and Hedgerows* and *Traditional Witchcraft for Woods and Forests. The Dictionary of Mystery & Magic* is also due for publication in 2012.

## Precious Stones

*Ruby, amethyst, emerald, diamond,*
*Sapphire, sardonyx, fiery-eyed carbuncle,*
*Jacynth, jasper, crystal a-sheen;*
*Topaz, turquoise, tourmaline, opal,*
*Beryl, onyx and aquamarine:-*
*Marvel, O mortal their hue, lustre, loveliness,*
*Pure as a flower when its petals unfurl*
*Peach-red carnelian, apple-green chrysoprase,*
*Amber and coral and orient pearl!*

**WALTER DE LA MARE**

# Introduction

Although *Magic Crystals, Sacred Stones* is drawn mainly from European and British geological findings, the same lessons can be learned about any area of the globe, since all the continents were originally joined together by the great equatorial landmass of Pangea some two hundred and fifty million years ago. Discover what geological formations make up your part of the world, and which different crystals and minerals are peculiar to those rocks. The magical and sacred uses of the stones may differ slightly between continents and cultures, but the fundamental makeup of the rocks from which they come remains eternal.

This book is dedicated to the memory of Mériém Clay-Egerton, herself a Doctor of Geology, who had a life-long passion for archaeology and anthropology, and who brought both art and science into the realms of magical teaching. These activities led to an even more intimate association with the Earth and its rock formations by active participation in caving and climbing. Together with her husband Bob, they founded the first cave rescue team in the Peak District, and are both still remembered with great respect in caving circles.

But the final word in this Introduction comes from the celebrated mineralogist, George Frederick Kunz: "The use of precious stones in early times as amulets and talismans is shown in many ancient records, and several scholars have assumed that this belief in the magic efficacy of stones gave rise to their use as objects of personal adornment."

Mélusine Draco
Galtee Mountains — 2010
Ireland

## Chapter One

# Time Span

In classical Greek mythology, Zeus being angered by the deeds of men, decided to destroy the whole of mankind by flood. Deucalion, a son of Prometheus, was warned by his father of the forthcoming Deluge and, with his wife Pyrrha, built a boat to ride out the storm. When the waters subsided, they found themselves on Mount Parnassus, where the oracle advised them to throw over their shoulders 'the bones of their mother'. Understanding this to refer to the stones of the Earth, they did as they were directed, and from the stones thrown by Deucalion there sprang up men, and from those thrown by Pyrrha, women. This is, of course, only one of the many global myths about the Deluge but from a magical perspective it is the earliest and most evocative one that identifies the sacred stones of the earth as the bones of the Earth Mother.

Closer to home, we know our ancestors began to utilise these 'bones' during the late Stone Age, when early man began to make stone hand-axes and later, to fashion razor-sharp blades from flint; the most sought-after raw material in antiquity being a volcanic glass called obsidian. And from there it was only a small step to creating items for personal adornment because man was now capable of perforating certain stones, which he wore openly on his person instead of carrying them about in a pouch, much as a shaman or medicine-man might.

Rocks are made up of specific combinations of minerals, and the endless ways in which these minerals combine results in the huge variety of rocks and landscapes we see in Nature. At this period of history, the geological impact on the lives of the people is also demonstrated by the relationship between prehistoric sites and their topographical settings. According to Christopher Tilley in *A Phenomenology of Landscape*, the architecture of Neolithic stone tombs focussed the attention on landscape features, such as rock outcrops, river valleys and mountain spurs in the immediate vicinity. And as each culture developed in different parts of the world, whatever rocks were found beneath their feet would become the building blocks for their sacred monuments.

The primitive associations with funerary customs and emerging ancestor worship were openly expressed by the recognition of some supernatural force that could influence or change the course of events. Of the sacredness of stones among peoples in the early stages of civilisation, Sir James Frazer (*The Golden Bough*) wrote extensively on the many examples from different cultures, especially of "the efficacy of such stones in the making of oaths". As civilisation slowly developed, colourful or translucent stones, would probably have acquired commonly recognised qualities and associations, observed Frank J. Anderson in *Riches of the Earth:* "Some worn as plaques or amulets, conferred the protection and guidance of supernatural beings, while others became the insignia of power and prestige. Jewellery had also evolved into both royal and ecclesiastical regalia."

Foreign traders were introducing all different kinds of 'stones' into Britain in the form of tools, jewellery and other artefacts, which demonstrates that the cutting, carving and importing of stones was already an established industry. For example, a jadite axe head found at the Neolithic Sweet Track site, was identified by experts at the British Museum as having its source at the foothills of the Alps. Baltic amber has been discovered at Gough's Cave, and archaeologist Francis Pryor asks whether some routes whereby this (and other) materials found their way to Britain were beginning to emerge as early as late glacial times.

Even from that very early time in man's history, the Earth's precious minerals were recognised as having a value that could be exploited and/or revered once they had been extracted from the rocks beneath their feet. The most visible examples of these minerals are stones and rocks and, with the notable exception of mercury, are heavy, hard and compact — solid masses that form the shapes we recognise as crystals. And a crystal is a substance that has a constant, regular shape, even when ground down into tiny particles, each individual particle *still* retains the shape of the original crystal it came from, which is all part of its magic.

Minerals are natural substances that form inside a variety of different rock types, and at present, there are nearly 3000 different named varieties. This number is always increasing — in fact, some 30 or more new minerals are discovered every year, while others are struck off the list once scientific analysis reveals they do not fulfil all the necessary criteria. When *all* the registered names of minerals are taken into account, they total nearly 15,000, including all the different types, variations and obsolete names. Of these, only about 30 are common at the Earth's surface, and make up the bulk of the rocks we can discover on our magical quest.

Dr Iain Stewart (*Journeys From the Centre of the Earth*) gives an excellent description of minerals as being collections of chemical elements organised in unique arrangements, just as certain letters make up words — and just as words are arranged into sentences, different sets of minerals grouped together in certain ways result in rocks. And regularly occurring combinations of minerals are the 'grammar' that produces the main rock types: limestone, sandstone, marble, granite and basalt.

Unfortunately, many writers in the 'mind, body and spirit' genre often fail to take the crystal's long metamorphosis into account; often giving the crystal attributes that are far removed from its original roots and early magical correspondences. If we wish to utilise the 'sympathetic' elements in the crystal for magical, mystical or medical reasons, then it is important to understand exactly what natural processes created the 'jewel' we hold in our hands, and why our ancestors held it to be sacred. So, let's go back to the beginning …

## The Forming of the Earth

The actual history of rocks has no clearly defined beginning, although science has assigned various 'geological periods' that represent a chapter in the story of the Earth, showing the stages of evolution and the development of the land-masses as we know them today. If we *really* wish to establish a magical link with these rocks, crystals and minerals, it helps to understand a little about their formation.

Firstly, we need to be able to identify the different types of rock that make up the Earth itself and to understand how each type fits together in the great scheme of things.

**Igneous rocks:**

Igneous rocks are crystalline or glassy rock formations that were originally created by the cooling and solidification of molten rock known as magma. This process originally took place deep beneath the surface of the Earth, but subsequent geological activity may have pushed igneous formations towards, and sometimes onto the surface of the Earth. The word 'igneous' comes from the Latin *ignis*, meaning 'fire', since magma may flow from volcanoes, or from long fissures as lava. When it reaches the surface, lava may be formed into pyroclastic rock, which are fragments ejected into the air during a volcanic explosion and range in size from dust particles to huge boulders. Often, however, magma cools and solidifies underground into intrusive igneous rocks, which may only come to the surface millions of years after they were formed, as a result of erosion, or tectonic plate processes. **Represented by Elemental Fire.**

**Metamorphic rocks:**
Metamorphism is the process by which pre-existing sedimentary and igneous rocks are 'mineralogically' and texturally altered by heat, pressure and chemically active fluids within the Earth. Dynamic metamorphism is caused by pressure alone; contact metamorphism is caused by heat given out by magma, as the heat bakes and changes the composition of the rocks; and regional metamorphism is caused by pressure and heat generated in areas where tectonic movement is pushing up mountains, and its effects can extend for hundreds of miles. Slate, marble and gneiss are examples of metamorphic rocks. **Represented by Elemental Earth.**

**Sedimentary rocks:**
The surface of the Earth is constantly changing as wind, water and ice relentlessly wear away at it. Each of these forces is capable of breaking down rock materials in their original location, carrying them over vast distances, and setting them down elsewhere. Among rocks that have been formed by these processes are chalk, clay, coal, limestone, sand, sandstone and shale: these are collectively known as sedimentary rocks. There are three main kinds of sedimentary rocks: clastic sedimentary rocks are formed from fragments worn from the land; chemical sedimentary rocks formed by chemical action and reaction; and organic sedimentary rocks, which is composed mostly of the remains of once-living organisms. **Represented by the duality of Elemental Air and Elemental Water.**

In later chapters, the terms 'metamorphosed' and 'altered' occur frequently in connection with the forming and transformation of stones and crystals due to pressure and heat — and what is meant by these terms is best explained by E. P. Bottley in *Rocks & Minerals:* "We know that deep mines get warmer the deeper we go — that the temperature of the earth increases as we go down by between 10° and 30° centigrade per kilometre ..." In fact, if limestone is heated deep in the earth, the pressure of the overlying rocks prevents any gas from escaping, and if just a small amount of carbon dioxide is driven into the pores and spaces that may be present, this helps to start far-reaching changes in the rock:

> *"The tiny chalk grains or the shelly fossils begin to be changed into clean, clear, uniformly-sized crystals of calcite. Eventually, given enough heat, the limestone will lose all trace of its original variations and become a homogeneous mass of calcite crystals — a marble ... Similarly, a sandstone may when deeply buried become re-crystallised into new quartz grains all interlocking with one another to make exceptionally hard and resilient rock quartzite."*

Another source of heat known to cause considerable change in the structure of the rocks stems from the pressure of large masses of granite being pushed into the 'crust' level. These molten rocks reached a temperature of some 700° or 800°C and have cooled down over hundreds of thousands of years. Rocks surrounding these hot bodies are 'altered', with the greatest changes occurring closest to the heat source. When heat to this extent has occurred, it is often difficult to recognise the original rocks as both sedimentary and igneous origins may have been completely blotted out. Metamorphic rocks may also be subject to a second phase of change, and in some cases, there is even evidence of several separate metamorphisms.

Not all changes to the Earth's surface, however, have resulted from primordial volcanic and earthquake disturbances. The 2004 *tsunami* disaster that claimed the lives of 125,000 people in the Indian Ocean was the result of colossal tectonic plate movement — but was mild by comparison. Nevertheless, the earthquake caused the Earth to wobble on its axis by an inch or so, altered regional geography by a few metres, and cut the length of the day by a few millionths of a second. It struck where one plate corresponding to the Indian Ocean floor is being pushed under another, along a fault line that stretches from the seabed to a few miles beneath the ocean floor, the two plates slipping violently and abruptly over a 700-mile stretch. A spokesman from the Earthquake Hazard Assessment Project said, "A piece of the Earth's crust is in a different place, though relative to the mass of the Earth it is tiny and the effects, though potentially just barely observable, will be small."

## Primordial Moving and Shaking

But back in the more turbulent past, while all this primordial moving and shaking was going on, the earliest forms of life were beginning to emerge into a hostile environment. The Earth was still far from settled, and every few million years another upheaval would alter the shape of the landmass, as we can see from the following:

The **Pre-Cambrian** era shows signs of soft jellyfish and worms; the limestone reveals the presence of algae in large reefs, the oldest of which may have lived more than 3,000 million years ago.

During **Cambrian** times, which lasted about 100 million years, there was no Atlantic Ocean as we know it and almost certainly Europe, Africa and the Americas were joined together to make the great equatorial landmass of Pangea. As a long, inland sea began to expand, the warm climate encouraged the abundant life-forms of shelled creatures and coral, whose calcareous skeletons formed a great thickness of limestone on the Cambrian sea floors. These creatures were not crude organisms but advanced animals like the trilobites, some of which were a foot long. Where the British Isles were located, "coarse pebbly deposits, finer sands and extremely fine silts and muds were poured into the sea, yielding the sandstones, siltstones and shales that can be found today in Wales and Scotland" (*A Fieldguide to Rocks & Minerals*).

The **Ordovician** period, which lasted for about 60 million years, saw earth movements reversing the process, which is shown by fossils from the times that are all marine: there is no sign of land-life, except for a few traces of primitive, armour-plated fish. In Britain, bursts of volcanic rocks poured into the seas.

During the **Silurian** age, lasting some 40 million years, the sandstones, limestones and shales gradually in-filled the seas in a similar way to happenings in the Ordovician and Cambrian periods. The fossils in the shale were still graptolites, but shells and corals were plentiful in the limestone, the Welsh borderland being an excellent source. It was during this period that huge belts of metamorphic rocks were created in Scotland, as enormous granite masses pushed their way up through the bedded rocks.

The magnificent boulder beds, known as 'old red sandstone', were formed during the **Devonian** period, lasting about 50 million years. By contrast, across southern England and southern Ireland, stretched a broad sea in which coral limestones, sandstones and shales were produced. In Britain, the mountain-building movements of the earth shifted the positions of land and sea.

The sea flooding in across the Devonian land mass created immense quantities of limestone packed with fossils of a colossal variety, forming the lower deposits of the **Carboniferous** period — which lasted about 80 million years. This sequence, repeated over and over again, created the great coal deposits of the Upper

Carboniferous period in Britain.

All the continents were definable by the **Permian** period (which lasted about 45 million years) and one of the greatest concentrations of snow and ice that spread across the landmass.

The **Triassic** period, lasting some 45 million years, saw red sandstone covering much of Britain; the pebbles it contained were being wind-blasted into wedge-shapes called 'dreikanters', which testify to the desert conditions that prevailed during this time.

The **Jurassic** period, (of some 45 million years duration) is best known for its spectacular dinosaur remains. By this time, warm shallow waters had covered the land and Britain swarmed with the low-jawed ichthyosaurs: remains of these animals have been found in the Jurassic strata of southern England. From this time, we have the pea-like oolites, pellets of chalk, often built around bits of shell or sand; the coiled shells of ammonites and the cone-shaped belemmites.

Similar creatures survived into the **Cretaceous** period, which lasted some 65 million years, and from the sea was formed the famous chalklands of southern England. At the end of the Cretaceous period, the giant retiles were totally wiped out, leaving the "explosive evolution of mammals in the following sixty million years" (*Geology & Scenery in England & Wales*) of the volcanic **Tertiary** and **Quaternary** periods.

The Earth has undergone some monumental changes from the Big Bang to the present day. The next time you hold a tiny crystal in your hand, muse upon the strange and wondrous journey it has undergone before finishing up as part of a display in the local occult shop ... because this is the *real* magical connection to crystals and sacred stones ... that should not be trivialised by superstition and fashionable fake-lore.

This magical journey, however, is not just about collecting pretty pebbles to enhance our homes. We must also become aware of the landscape beneath our feet, for this plays an important part in harnessing the 'Earth energies' that are an integral part of all magical working.

**Try this exercise:**
When sitting on a garden seat or park bench look at the stones around your feet. At first glance this will probably appear as ordinary gravel, or aggregate from a builders' merchant or garden centre — smooth pebbles or rough-quarried stone. Having said that, pebbles and stones are to be found every-where: in the shallow streambed, on the sandy banks of an inland river, turned over in a ploughed field, on the beach, or even dug up our own gardens. It isn't necessary to acquire a degree in geology to collect 'magical' pebbles because our choice is reliant on a small stone that catches our eye because of its unusual colour or shape regardless of what it is.

- Each stone may be discovered under unusual circum-stances, or it may be something that we just feel the need to pick up and possess. Whatever the reason for our selection, these stones will begin to form the basis for our magical collection. Take your time and add one from a different location whenever you see or feel something special.

- Because these small stones are 'special', you will remember exactly where and under what circumstances you found them. **This is important**. Keep them together in a tall glass jar or goldfish bowl until you have sufficient quantity to utilise for magical use. Keep a note of each one in a magical journal or diary if you have a poor memory.

- You may even be lucky enough to find a 'hagstone' — a small stone that has a hole bored through it naturally by water, weather erosion, or by a small marine creature that burrows its way into rock.

- Invest in a beginner's field guide to rocks and minerals and you may find that you've discovered a fascinating hobby, as well as enhancing your magical ability.

Remember this Chinese story about a peasant who asked a wise man to help him find great quantities of gemstones. "If that is your wish," replied the sage, "even the pebbles in the sea will become gemstones." The simple truth is that a gemstone is considered precious only if someone wishes to own it.

# Chapter Two

# Imago Mundi

In the first chapter, we saw how the British Isles (and other landmasses) were formed and re-formed over millions of years, and now we will turn our attention to the forming of the landscape. Regardless of where we live in the world, however, some geological formations are better suited for magical working than others, an idea that was mooted by Dion Fortune in her novel, *The Goat-Foot God*. ... "Now the best place to get the kind of experiences you want is on chalk. If you think of it, all the earliest civilisation in these islands was on the chalk ... Avebury's on the chalk; and St Albans is on the chalk ..."

We could cheat, of course, and home-in on those famous ancient sites but as Fortune also pointed out, these power-centres have all been 'exorcised' long ago by the tramp of the idly curious and besides, we need to travel much further back in time to understand *why* they became power-centres in the first place. *A Phenomenology of Landscape* gives a detailed overview of the topographic features of the prehistoric landscape that attracted our distant ancestors' attention: an affinity with the coast; mountain escarpments and spurs; the ridges, valleys and chalk downlands. The latter including the Dorset Cursus, which was one of the two most spectacular monuments in Neolithic Britain, only rivalled in size and the sheer scale of its construction by the earthworks on nearby Hambleton Hill.

The author, Christopher Tilley, poses the question of why particular locations were chosen for the erection of these sacred stone monuments as opposed to others. This type of analysis has hardly been explored in any detail, but he suggests that the symbolics of landscape and the role of social memory influenced the choice of site location:

> *"People do not deliberately occupy inhospitable habitats ... by virtue of some slavish accommodation to a symbolic scheme; but the places that they do occupy take on, through time, particular sets of meanings and connotations which are at least partially inter-pretable from archaeological evidence and appear to be too important to be ignored."*

The results appear to suggest that ancestral connections between the living population of Mesolithic hunter-gatherers and the past were embodied in the 'Being' of the landscape and an emotional attachment to 'Place' (both of which we would now identify with the *genius loci*), to which they repeatedly returned during their seasonal nomadic life-style. Later Neolithic people "actively appropriated these ancestral powers and meanings" (*A Phenomenology of Landscape* ) with the construction of chambered tombs and huge stone monuments. These monuments provided the first focal points of emerging belief and visibly brought the presence of the ancestral past into what was then, contemporary public consciousness.

Needless to say, regardless of where we live in the world, this type of ancient site reveals *where* our indigenous ancestors located those power-places that were to become the focus of subsequent religious beliefs. Some were designated as burial sites; others the sites for great earthen mounds, many of which were displaced by huge stone monuments — and very much later by magnificent churches and cathedrals. Obviously, the most important aspect of each site being **not what is seen above ground, but the geological formation beneath our feet**.

## The Chalklands

Dion Fortune was, of course, one of the most accomplished of 20th century occultists and in his biography about her magical career (*Priestess*), Alan Richardson reveals that the *mise en scène* for her novel *The God-Foot God,* was an actual farm house location: "There was an energy along this line, an energy which was preserved in the chalk stratum on which Monks Farm was built, much like the energy that could (and can) be felt in the outcrops of carboniferous limestones on the Ormes, on Brean Down, and Glastonbury Tor."

Chalk is a very pure limestone formed from marine sediments, and its name is derived from the Latin *calx*, meaning 'limestone', a word that in turn comes from the Greek *khalix*, meaning 'a pebble'. Chalk is abundant in many parts of the world and because so much of it was formed between 140 and 65 million years ago that this whole geological period has now been named after it: the word Cretaceous comes from the Latin *creta*, a word which literally means 'Cretan earth' because the Greek island of Crete is so rich in this sedimentary rock.

Apart from limestone, the main components of chalk are the fossilised remains of tiny marine organisms such as coccoliths (a species of plankton) and foraminifers (protozoa that resembles tiny shellfish). Most of the fossils in chalk can only be seen with the aid of a microscope, some however *are* readily visible to the naked eye, and these provide a wealth of information about life on Earth before recorded history. Many chalk deposits contain other sedimentary formations such as flint and marcasite, also useful to the magical practitioner.

As most chalk formed through sedimentary deposits in marine environments during the Cretaceous Period, it contains no mud or silt because the surrounding landmasses were hot, dry, low-lying deserts, and not fed by rivers. Some of the world's most famous chalk deposits are found in southern England, across the Weald (Kent and Sussex) and the white cliffs of Dover on the shore of the English Channel. Elsewhere, extensive chalk layers are found in Count Antrim (Northern Ireland), the Dolomites (Italy) and Wyoming (USA) — all ideal places for locating powerful earth energies.

And among the inhabited chalk-land regions of prehistoric England, none was more important than Salisbury Plain, with its system of track-ways leading to the Plain from several parts of the south and east coasts. This region shows more signs of early occupation of different dates than almost any other area with its ancient track-ways, its hill top camps, its tumuli and its magnificent stone monuments.

## Magical correspondences

Because of the high content of its marine origins and the established channelling of Otherworld energies, we can safely assign chalk to the **Element of Water**. Or more precisely, the '**Earthy part of Water**' symbolised by the Princess of Cups in the Tarot, who represents the power of Water to give sustenance to idea, to support life, and form the basis of chemical metamorphism (transformation) as silently and effortlessly she goes about her work.

| | |
|---|---|
| **Mineral:** | Sulphates |
| **Gemstone:** | Beryl; Aquamarine |
| **Colour:** | Deep blue; White, flecked purple (like mother of pearl); Deep olive green; Sea green |
| **Magical Powers:** | The Great Work; Talismans; Crystal gazing |
| **Magical Weapon:** | The Cup or Chalice |

When undertaking magical working on chalk, we should use these correspondences to enhance the pursuit of The Great Work, to give added power to our talismans and for the development in the art of crystal gazing.

**If we are unable to connect with chalk because of the environment where we live, then we need to acquire a piece of flint that will contain all the necessary properties and magical**

associations. **Keep this in a small pouch and do not attempt any form of cleansing, as this will remove all the qualities for which this particular piece was chosen. The flint should be obtained from a natural site and not bought from a shop or mail order. Treat the acquisition of this stone as part of your magical quest.**

## Limestone

Limestone is one of the Earth's most widespread rock formations and in its purest form it is white, grey, cream or yellow — impure or weathered varieties may appear black, brown or red — and nearly all limestone contains fossils. Although limestone appears in many shapes and sizes, it all originated in one of two ways. One form (autochthonous) originates from seawater and typically contains the fossilised remnants of many living organisms. The other (allochthonous) is formed when pre-existent limestone becomes dislodged from its original location and is re-deposited elsewhere by glacial movement, floodwater and landslips.

The most spectacular sites are the so-called 'limestone pavements' similar to those found near Malham in the Yorkshire Dales (England). These are horizontal layers on the Earth's surface, especially when on fairly exposed ground, forming this particular geological feature. Over millions of years, this flat sheet of rock is weathered and eroded by wind, rain, water, ice and snow until it develops the distinctive pattern of ridges (clints) and clefts (grykes).

The harder limestone, being so resistant to weather as to produce ranges of lofty hills, is called Mountain Limestone. It helps to form the 'backbone of England' (the Pennine Chain) and builds the Peaks and Fells of Derbyshire, and the Mendip Hills. It also occurs in Wales, around the Lake District and Scottish Lowlands, and occupies a wide area in central Ireland.

## Magical correspondences

Because of the highly visible surface rocks creating the hills, peaks and fells reaching up to the sky, we can safely assign limestone to the **Element of Air**. Or more precisely, the '**Earthy part of Air**' symbolised by the Princess of Swords in the Tarot, who represents the influence of Heaven upon Earth; she is firm and aggressive, with 'great practical wisdom and subtlety in material things'.

| | |
|---|---|
| **Mineral:** | None given |
| **Gemstone:** | Topaz; Chalcedony |
| **Colour:** | Bright pale yellow; Emerald flecked gold; Blue emerald green; Sky blue |
| **Magical Powers:** | Divination |
| **Magical Weapon:** | The Dagger or Fan |

When undertaking magical working on limestone, we should use these correspondences to focus and enhance our powers of divination, since the element brings us closer to 'god'.

**If we are unable to connect with limestone because of the environment where we live, then we need to acquire a fossil that will contain all the necessary properties and magical associations. Keep this in a pouch and do not attempt any form of cleansing, as this will remove all the qualities for which this particular piece was chosen. The fossil should be obtained from a natural limestone site and not bought from a shop or mail order. Treat the acquisition of this stone as part of your magical quest.**

## Face of Granite

Granite is an igneous rock that originates at great depth through the solidification of magma, and is subsequently exposed to the Earth's surface by the erosion of less resistant, overlying rocks.

Despite its dramatic origins, this is one of the most widespread crystalline rock formations on the surface of the Earth — and probably the most magical, having been used for sculpture and sacred buildings since the dawn of history. The name comes from the Latin *granum*, which refers to the coarse grains that are its most striking and consistent physical characteristic.

Granite has a mottled appearance and is usually white, light grey, pink or yellowish in colour. Closer inspection reveals a jumbled mass of tiny crystals, some almost too small and some large enough to be visible; here and there it may also include larger crystals several inches long; and at least three entirely different types of crystal are distinguishable.

- The predominant type that gives the rock its colour consists of **feldspar** from the German for 'field crystal'. This mineral may be white or pink.

- The sparkle in the granite comes from specks of black **mica** (from the Latin for 'shining').

- Quartz is a form of silica and its crystals are more irregular, giving the appearance of having filled the spaces between the other two after the rock had been formed.

Granite also contains a wide range of other mineral species. The essential ingredients — without which the rock does not merit the name — are biotite mica, microcline, muscovite mica ortho-clase, quartz and plagioclase feldspar. The accessory minerals often found in granite are allanite, apatite, ilmenite, pyrite and zircon — while others may sometimes include members of the garnet group, topaz and tourmaline. All grist to the magical practitioner's mill.

Granite is most commonly found in exposed formations that may cover hundreds of thousands of square miles, and the most extensive zones are located in the great pre-Cambrian shields across the globe. One spot that has proved itself to be particularly strong on magical energies is the granite outcrop at Markfield (Charwood Forest in Leicestershire) that rises unexpectedly from the Midlands clay plain. These rocks are more closely comparable with those of many parts of Wales and represent some of the oldest rocks known anywhere in England.

On the western side of the central plain, the magical character of the Malvern Hills is also unlike any other outcrop in England and Wales, and may represent a slice of pre-Cambrian base-rock, which is otherwise found at the surface only in north-west Scotland. The eastern face of this range is very steep and may have resulted from a movement that pushed up the ancient floor and brought pre-Cambrian rocks up against the New Red Sandstone causing an overlap of the latter onto the older rocks (as at Charnwood Forest).

## Magical correspondences

Dominating the landscape from rugged mountain ranges to the sophisticated pyramids of Egypt, granite comes from the igneous rocks, which the Greeks equated with fire, so we can safely assign granite to the **Element of Fire**. Or more precisely, the '**Earthy part of Fire**' symbolised by the Princess of Wands in the Tarot, who represents the 'irresistible chemical attraction of the combustible substance'.

| | |
|---|---|
| **Mineral:** | Nitrates |
| **Gemstone:** | Fire Opal |
| **Colour:** | Glowing orange-scarlet; Vermillion, flecked crimson and emerald; Scarlet flecked gold; Vermillion |
| **Magical Powers:** | Evocation, Pyromancy |
| **Magical Weapon:** | Wand or Lamp |

When undertaking magical working on granite, we should use these correspondences to focus and enhance our powers of divination through pyromancy, and the evocation of fire elementals.

**If we are unable to connect with granite because of the environment where we live, then we need to acquire a piece of rock that will contain all the necessary properties and magical associations. Keep this in a pouch and do not attempt any form of cleansing, as this will remove all the qualities for which this particular piece was chosen. The granite should be obtained from a natural site and not bought from a shop or mail order. Treat the acquisition of this stone as part of your magical quest.**

## Sandstone

Sandstone (sometimes known as arenite from the Latin meaning 'sand') is another sedimentary rock composed mainly of sand-sized minerals or rock grains of quartz and/or feldspar because these are the most common minerals in the Earth's crust. Like sand, sandstone may be any colour, but the most common colours are tan, brown, yellow, red, gray, pink, and white depending on the presence of iron, or with a greenish hue that comes from the mineral glauconite. The natural cement that binds the sandstone into solid rock may consist of clay, ironstones, limestone — or silica. Sandstones cemented together by silica are so hard as to demand a special name: quartzite.

Since sandstone beds often form highly visible cliffs and other topographic features, certain colours of sandstone have been strongly identified with certain regions. The rock is composed of grains of pre-existent geological material that has been transported by water and wind, and deposited in a new location. Some of the finest sites are found in Australia, central Europe, the USA and north Wales.

Splits in the rock may reveal undulations or ripple-marks, like those produced by the waves on a beach. Other surfaces are marked with rain-prints, the tiny pits formed on a bygone sea-beach by falling drops of rain. Others again bear the traces of crawling sea-creatures, or the footprints of animals or birds, or even the marks produced by the tips of swaying seaweed-fronds.

## Magical correspondences

Despite being easily weathered, sandstone has been used by builders and sculptors for thousands of years, including the ancient ruins of Petra (Jordan), which has been described poetically as 'a rose-red city half as old as time'. The disadvantages of sandstone are out-weighted by its natural beauty and the ease with which it can be shaped and carve into outstanding works of art such as the famous bust of Queen, Nefertiti that has survived more or less intact since it was carved during the Egyptian 18th Dynasty.

Because it is highly susceptible to weathering and decomposition, and ultimately crumbling to dust, we can safely assign sandstone to the **Element of Earth**. Or more precisely, the '**Earthy part of Earth**' symbolised by the Princess of Disks in the Tarot, who represents the 'element of the brink of Transfiguration'. She has been depicted with her sceptre descending into the Earth where the point becomes a diamond and her shield denoting the 'twin spiral forces of Creation in perfect equilibrium'.

| | |
|---|---|
| **Mineral:** | Bismuth |
| **Gemstone:** | Salt |
| **Colour:** | Citrine, olive, russet and black; black flecked yellow; Dark brown; Amber |
| **Magical Powers:** | Alchemy; Geomancy; Making of Pantacles |
| **Magical Weapon:** | The Pantacle or Salt |

When undertaking magical working on sandstone, we should use these correspondences to focus and enhance our alchemical powers, geomancy and the making of magical or sacred symbols.

**If we are unable to connect with sandstone because of the environment where we live, then we need to acquire a piece of quartzite that will contain all the necessary properties and magical associations. Keep this in a pouch and do not attempt any form of cleansing, as this will remove all the qualities for which this particular piece was chosen. The quartzite should be obtained from a natural site and not bought from a shop or mail order. Treat the acquisition of this stone as part of your magical quest.**

## Basalt

A fine-grained, sometimes glassy basic igneous rock. Most of the recent volcanoes, and many of the older ones, now erupt lava that solidifies to a fine-grained black rock, composed largely of microscopic grains of feldspar, pyroxene and olivine — but no quartz. Basalts are generally found in lava flows that may be extensive and often erupted from fissures and vents. It is widely distributed throughout the earth's crust, both on the continental landmass, and beneath the ocean beds.

In many parts of the world basalt flows form great piles, tens of thousands of feet thick, as for example in Iceland, Mull, the Deccan of India and the Columbia River area — not to mention the Giant's Causeway in Ireland, Fingal's Cave in the Hebridian islands, and the mysterious statues carved from local basaltic rock formations on Easter Island.

A curious feature of basalt is its 'unwillingness to be ground down from a boulder to a pebble'. Its hardness and compactness help it to withstand for a very long period of time, the tumbling of stream, river and tide, although it has a tendency to break up into fragments before it can be reduced to pebble size. Although basalt is the most widely distributed rock on the surface of the earth, basalt pebbles are few and far between.

## Magical correspondences

Basalt rocks are also found on the Moon, and samples revealed that lunar basalts, like terrestrial varieties of the same rock, were originally produced by volcanic activity. Unlike terrestrial rocks, lunar basalt is not susceptible to the normal rock cycle, and remains almost exactly as it was when it originally solidified from lava. With all these properties in mind, we can safely assigned basalt to the **Root of the Powers of Fire, Earth, Air and Water** and the **Court Cards** of the Tarot: Lord of the Flame and the Lightening, Lord of the Wild and Fertile Land, Lord of the Winds and Breezes, and Lord of the Waves and the Waters.

| | |
|---|---|
| **Mineral:** | Carbon |
| **Gemstone:** | Black diamond |
| **Colour:** | White merging into grey; the seven prismatic colours; deep purple, nearly black. |
| **Magical Powers:** | Invisibility, Transformation, Vision of the Genius. |
| **Magical Weapon:** | Intelligence |

When undertaking a magical working on basalt we should use these correspondences to focus on, and enhance our concept of Knowledge, Wisdom and Understanding. If it is possible, we should obtain a polished black egg made from basalt to aid us in the Great Work.

**If we are unable to connect with basalt because of the environment where we live, then we need to acquire a piece that will contain all the necessary properties and magical associations. Keep this in a pouch and do not attempt any form of cleansing, as this will remove all the qualities for which this particular piece was chosen. Where possible, the basalt should be obtained from a natural site and not bought from a shop or mail order (unless it is a polished egg-shaped stone, which**

**must be cleansed). Treat the acquisition of this stone as part of your magical quest.**

There are, of course many other rocks that make up the Earth's surface and each of them will have certain positive or negative *magical* properties. As an example, we will look at what has been found to be the best and the worst when it comes to drawing from, or stifling, magical energy.

**The Best** — Slate is a widespread, metamorphic rock that forms through the alteration of sedimentary material at relatively low temperatures and pressure. It is commonly found inter-layered with sedimentary strata and with rocks of volcanic origin; usually grey or black, but may also appear in shades of blue, brown, buff or green. Its name derives from the French *esclat*, meaning 'fragment'.

- Once we understand that quartz is very abundant in slate and may form as much as 70% by weight of the rock, it is not difficult to see why this particular material generates so much Earth energy. Magical and psychic working on slate packs a very distinctive punch, especially if the slate layers are close to the surface.

**The Worst** — Clay is classically white, but may also appear in almost any colour — especially black, blue, brown, dark green, grey or red. The name derives from the Old English *clæg* meaning 'sticky'. It is a widespread sedimentary rock with grains too small to be seen under any but the most powerful microscope, and may form in many different geological environments throughout the world. The most extensive layers are found in both deep and shallow marine deposits, in moraines (piles of debris) left behind by receding glaciers, and in zones of pre-existent rocks (especially granite) that have been altered by hydrothermal fluids.

- Try walking through heavy clay and it immediately becomes apparent why Earth energy is often 'blocked' or sluggish. Magical working on clay involves a lot of magical generating techniques by the practitioner, and unless there is a considerable amount of experience (knowledge) to draw on, things may take a long time to come to fruition.

Like all things magical, however, nothing is as simple, or precise, as it seems. Just as the outcome in all magical and psychic exercises depend on the *personal chemistry of the individual*, so the blend of individuality, ability and Earth energies can combine to produce the most extraordinary results. And some things work better than others ...

## Eternal Quartz

It is the quartz element of granite that reconnects us with the spirit within the landscape. As an accomplished occultist and having a doctorate in geology, Mériém Clay-Egerton was fascinated by the fact that for millennia humanity and quartz had interacted with each other. She wrote that our ancestors having recognised the qualities of quartz was evident from the studies of its usage, not region by region, but over the entire area of the British Isles: "Everywhere one looks there are clear distinct traces. To people who know its potential, it was clearly no accidental employment of any material to hand. It was sought out for use. Why?"

Quartz is the most common constituent of rock, she went on to explain, a basic silicate dioxide having three molecules arranged in either a right or left-handed spiral form, which has the power of polarising light in more than one direction:

*"When light enters a crystal it splits into two beams, due to the*

*differing speeds of the light's velocity being refracted back from the different vibration of the crystal's lattices, and their own individual refracting indices. In certain circumstances, the crystals can act as 'windows' to ultra-violet and infra-red wavelengths. In addition to these scientific points, we may also hear quartz crystals hum or 'sing'. We can also see quartz crystals displaying piezo-electric effects."*

These are scientific terms for what our ancestors saw or knew:

*"Burial chambers with quartz kerb-stones were commonplace, as were the pits used for inhumations, which were sprinkled with quartz chippings, both whole and broken. There is a school of thought that these were used to either keep the individuals concerned safely at rest, or to permit the living to contact spirit entities when they were in a correctly attuned state."*

On a magical level, Mériém Clay-Egerton wrote:

*"Standing stones (some of which are made of quartz, others may contain a high percentage of it), are accepted by psychics [and magical practitioners] as being able to act as conductors of 'earth-force', such as that encountered at nodal points for energy lines. If they are acting like natural 'acupuncture needles', then it is not surprising that they should be as pure a substance as possible and with natural powers of their own. Many circles in the south-west of England appear to have been originally constructed with a central point; other phases being tacked on afterwards. A quartz stone, or stones with high quartz content, will often appear in such a prominent position, having superseded the original wooden post."*

And much closer to home:

*"Nowadays, we protect our water with chemicals to make it fit for us to drink, but in ancient times folk made offerings to the guardians of holy wells. Some were simple things, others were valuable objects that had been ceremoniously broken; it is strange how often white stones, and quartz in particular, figured highly on the list of offerings. As the wells were quite often used in fertility and healing rites, then I suppose we should naturally expect quartz to be a frequent gift. Today, crystal healing is still practised; and quartz plain or coloured, is one of the principal stones used — yet another relic of our past."*

On a final note: quartz is solid silica and if it did not crystallise when it solidified it is known as flint, and everyone knows that two flints struck together will produce a spark. What is not generally known is that all quartz pebbles will do the same and often produce bigger and better sparks. Clear quartz, or rock crystal, will produce an orange spark if two pieces are struck together in a darkened room, together with the smell of burning and this can be viewed as magical fire from the very Earth itself

**Even if you feel a tremendous empathy with a particular site, NEVER be tempted to commit an act of desecration by chipping bits off the stones or monument, since these will NOT enhance your magical or meditational workings — and may even have an adverse effect.**

## Nature's Jewel Case

Mountains are the places where rocks and minerals have been brought up from deep within the Earth's crust, in many cases deep from within the mantle of the planet's interior where metals and gemstones are formed. Most gemstones are minerals that form in the crust or upper mantle alongside metals, and brought to the surface along similar pathways. In fact, it is the *metallic elements acting as impurities* in the gems that give most their colour.

Emerald, garnet, jade, turquoise and amethyst were all mined in antiquity in the eastern Mediterranean by the ancient Egyptians, while lapis lazuli was imported from it natural home in Iran and Afghanistan. Although gem quality opal was highly prized by the Greeks and Romans, it was incredibly rare because it results from hundreds of millions of years of tropical weathering; diamonds being only found in the ancient interiors of the great land-masses such as Australia and southern Africa.

On a more humble level, semi-precious stones are broken away by the wind and rain from mountain peaks, and tumbled down into the river valleys, to be carried away to the shore. Quartz is one of the most popular of 'crystals' and pebbles having quartz as their dominant constituent are to be found on almost every beach, the differences in colour and appearance due to varying amounts of other minerals in each one, and also the way in which the quartz has formed.

Coloured varieties of rock crystal can be found on certain kinds of beach, the best known being amethyst, which is transparent to semi-transparent, purple to pale pink, with some white banding. Citrine is transparent to semi-transparent and golden yellow, while smoky quartz is deep yellow to brown. A variety of quartz that did not form large crystals when it cooled is known as chalcedony; it has a waxy lustre, is translucent, and has a milky-white, blue, gray or pale brown colour. The red variety, carnelian, glows with a warm fire when held up to the light and soon catches the eye on a sunny day near the water's edge: the colours vary from pale to deep red.

Despite all the wealth of the world, for the magical practitioner, natural quartz should remain the most precious gift of all.

## Try this exercise

Obtain a detailed geological map and/or reference book for the part of the world in which you live (i.e. *Geology & Scenery in England and Wales* by A. E. Truman for the UK) and chart the *precise* identity of the ground under your feet both at home and play. Most areas are made up of sheets of sedimentary rock laid down on the floor of some ancient sea, but in others, there are also sheets of lava and other rocks of igneous character. Many of these have been bent, crumpled and broken at different times owing to the great movements in the earth's crust, causing the edges of the sheets to reach the surface at various different angles.

- Wherever we live, there are hill-forms that also reflect the underlying structure and their origin is apparent in their shape. One clue is the fact that in many of the different regions the native stone has given a distinctive character to the local buildings

- Once you have located what appears be a suitable site, try to pinpoint your own personal energy spot by using a pendulum that contains an element of quartz. Dowse the site thoroughly and calculate where the energy is the strongest from the pendulum's reaction (see the exercise at the end of Chapter Four).

- If the location seems unsuitable for magical working, then a short journey of just a few hundred yards might make all the difference. For example: the short distance between the clay plain levels at Charnwood, and the granite outcrop is only a daily dog's walk away from each other.

The surrounding landscape will influence the way magical workings come to fruition, and also the amount of effort needed to be put into the ritual to bring about the desired effect. By understanding what lies beneath our feet will enhance our magical ability, and here we can learn to plug-in to the natural energy of the place

## Chapter Three

# Transcendental Variations

The earliest examples of gem-cutting and carving date back to the ancient cultures of Assyria, Babylon and Egypt, although according to *Encyclopaedia Britannica*, the date of around 500 BC marks the beginning of a period of great artistic taste and skill in gem engraving that extended throughout the ancient civilised world, and lasted until the 3$^{rd}$ or 4$^{th}$ century AD:

> *"With the Renaissance, the art of gem carving revived, and the engravers from that time produced results that equal the best Greek and Roman work; copies of ancient gem carvings made by some of the 18$^{th}$ century masters are distinguishable from true antiques only by experts of great proficiency."*

Until the 16$^{th}$ century, minerals and gemstones were listed in 'lapidaries' — a document in which the characteristics and properties of the minerals were described in great detail. The earliest surviving text is contained in a monumental encyclopaedia *Naturalis Historia*, compiled by Pliny the Elder in the 1$^{st}$ century AD, and was imitated by writers on the subject throughout the Middle Ages. Some versions listed both the magical and medicinal properties of the minerals and gemstones; others revealed the astrological significance, while others gave the religious symbolism of the stones.

The term 'lapidary', refers to either a book classifying stones, or the gemmologist, goldsmith or stonecutter himself, and by the Middle Ages there were dozens of books on the subject, although the most popular were translations from the Arabic, which focussed on the efficacy of precious stones as amulets. In

Alexandria, collections of books on gemstones were common-place among the fraternity of glasscutters and stone-engravers, and some of the titles have come down to us today.

- *The Book of Stones*, was believed to have been written by Aristotle (384–322BC), and examined the magical powers of gemstones, later being translated into Hebrew and Latin.

- *Materia Medica* of Dioscurides (1st century AD) records some two hundred 'stones' from a medicinal point of view, and although the majority are oxides and other minerals, a few authentic gems are also included. He served as a doctor in the Roman army during the reign of Nero.

- *De Lapidibus*, written by the one-time bishop, Marbode of Rennes (1035–1123) set forth the lore and uses of some 60 stones.

- *The Flowers of Knowledge of Stones*, written by the alchemist Shihab al-Din al-Tifashi of Cairo around 1154.

- *Lapidario*, the most famous of all gem books, was compiled by Alfonso X of Castile in the 13th century.

- *Gemmarum at Lapidum Historia* was compiled by Anselm Boethius (a doctor to Rudolph II of Prague) in 1609, and was probably the most important history of gems and stones of that century.

One of the most popular works in the Middle Ages, Marbode's work gathered all the pertinent matter about the powers inherent in stones that had been written from antiquity until the bishop's own time. Over 140 manuscripts of the treatise exist in the major libraries of Europe, and 18 printed editions have been published between 1511 and 1977. "Although its medical value is nil, Marbode's book can still tell us much about symbolism, medieval names for a variety of stones, and the psychological processes of the people of his era", writes Frank J. Anderson in *Riches of the Earth*.

As we can see, the belief in the magical and healing properties of stones and crystals has a *very* long history, with the lapidaries of the ancient world falling into those two main classes — the medicinal, and the magical, the latter often showing a strong astrological influence. But this was not primitive superstition. Those who compiled the lapidaries were the men of intellect and knowledge of their time — the power of gemstones was a very real science as far as they were concerned.

## Fake-Lore and Fraud

There are modern shops selling glass 'crystal' balls and crystal spheres made from ground and reconstituted material, but what we are looking at here are the fakes and frauds of Nature. Much of this fakery is man-made, although there is a surprising amount of it to be found on our beaches — the five main offenders that can be confused with pebbles are: brick, concrete, earthenware, china and glass. The ceaseless pounding of the waves and the grinding action of the sand can wear fragments of these materials to pebble-shapes in a very short time, warns Edward Fletcher in his modern lapidary, *Pebble Polishing:* "Corners are knocked off, surfaces smoothed, colours bleached, and a deceptive costing given to the finished shape. Even geologists can be confused."

Brick retains its colour of red or yellow and may often be mistaken for sandstone or jasper — scratch it with a knife and if it scrapes easily it is not jasper. Sandstone pebbles stay wet and are often found above the waterline — still moist when other pebbles nearby are quite dry. Although some are coarse-gained and others fine, sandstone differs from brick because of the tiny cavities in the made-made material — the only valley this piece has tumbled through will be Marsden Valley Brick Company! Pebbles of concrete should also be discarded, unless there is some interesting mineral embedded in the small fragment.

Earthenware and china can also be mistaken for sandstone but again, a scrape with a knife will reveal the true nature of the material. Sandstone is soft and crumbly, whereas hard-baked china and earthenware will be much tougher. And glass pebbles do not resemble the bottle glass from which they were formed, warns Fletcher: "Whether clear or coloured, they will be dramatically changed. All glassiness will have disappeared and they will have a frosted, crystalline appearance — very much like pure quartz, or some colourful semi-precious stone." Break off a fragment with a knife and if there is an obvious 'glassiness' underneath then glass it is — you would be unable to break off a fragment with a knife blade if it is quartz.

**Warning: However appealing these 'finds' may be, none have any magical value whatsoever**.

## The Science and Art of Geology

As George Frederick Kunz (*The Curious Lore of Precious Stones*) observes, "the magi, the wise men and the seers, the astrologers of the ages gone by found much in the matter of gems that we have nearly come close to forgetting". But according to the *Encyclopaedia Britannica*, the earliest beginnings of *geological* thought, like those of many other sciences, are mixed up with myth and legend, and vague cosmical speculations:

> "*It also happens that the Mediterranean basin, the home of many of the early civilisations whose written records have come down to us, is an area in which geological phenomena are peculiarly well displayed and striking; and it may well be a matter of wonder that the acute thinkers of antiquity did not manage to arrive at a more*

*reasonable and more correct interpretation of the facts than they did. It is perhaps worth remembering that geology even in its modern forms depends far less on complicated instruments and appliances than almost any other science. It is nearly all naked-eye observation of things on a large scale, and therefore might have been thought peculiarly well adapted to development in an early stage of civilisation."*

It wasn't until the 20th century that there was a tremendous upsurge of interest in geology by laymen and schoolchildren, which coincided with a period of great development in the earth sciences, especially in the application of new techniques, and the in-depth study of many older disciplines. As Kunz concludes, however, our scientific knowledge of cause and effect may prevent us from accepting many of the fanciful notions of the physicians and astrologers of the olden time but "surely no pleasure can be more innocent and justifiable than that inspired by the possession of beautiful natural objects."

## Talismans & Amulets — Part One

As Kunz also points out, the use of precious and semi-precious gemstones from early times as talismans and amulets is shown in many ancient records, and scholars have tended to believe that the magical efficacy of the stones gave rise to their later use as personal adornment: "Fetishism in all its forms depends upon an imperfect conception of what constitutes life and conscious being, so that will and thought are attributed to inanimate objects."

From an early date, the Christian church condemned the use of amulets as 'fetters of the soul' and preached against this pagan superstition, although it was later permissible to carry relics of the saints, or medallions blessed by the priest. The amulets of the Jews differed from those of the Christians, because Mosaic Law forbade the representation of human or animal form, and Jewish people were only permitted to wear or carry amulets engraved with characters of mystic or symbolic significance.

From the Middle Ages to the 17$^{th}$ century, people of all classes and stations accepted a belief in the talismanic virtues of gemstones — by the learned as well as the ignorant. The widely accepted 'doctrine of sympathy' (and, in some cases, antipathy) governed the belief that certain stones were influenced by a person's health, or even susceptible to the private thoughts of the wearer.

For example, turquoise *is* affected to a certain extent by bodily secretions, but popular superstition saw the phenomena reflected in other stones not possessing the same 'virtues' as the turquoise, and contributed to the concept that a magical sympathy existed between the stone and the wearer. Ralph Waldo Emerson's poem, 'The Amulet' could be used as a charm when preparing a stone for romance:

*Give me an amulet*
*That keeps intelligence with you —*
*Red when you love, and rosier red,*
*And when you love not, pale and blue.*

The magical virtue of a talisman or amulet, however, is not in the object itself, but in the suggestion of what it represents and incorporates, that gives the stone its power. And although the idea or symbol is nothing in itself, the real magical power is in its relation to the suggestion or idea it typifies. This goes a long way to explain much of the use of Hebrew symbolism in Western ritual magic and the magical Qabalah, because Mosaic Law only permitted amulets engraved with characters of mystic or symbolic significance.

## Try this exercise

The temptation to collect too many pebbles from a single site is often hard to resist — especially when we find ourselves on a shingle beach with millions of colourful stones glistening in the sunlight — but we must learn discipline. We are attempting to put together a magical collection and so the stones and their location must be as diverse as possible.

- For magic use, always collect small pebbles between the size of your thumbnail and the top joint of your thumb. To begin with, we all make the same mistake of trying to find near-perfect round pebbles but what we should be looking for are ovoids and discs, as well as the weird and wonderful.

- Each stone should mean something — and easily identified, because no two pebbles are exactly alike. There are always minute differences in hardness and mineral content that makes every pebble unique.

- The weird and wonderful can often include small hagstones, or pebbles that have split in half — leaving one side smooth and the other a rough domed surface like a natural Egyptian scarab. These can form part of your collection or be kept separate as personal charms.

Larger stones that take your fancy can be taken home for use as paper-weights or doorstops; any egg-shaped stone would make a good 'worry-stone' to reduce stress if it can easily be tumbled from palm to palm.

# Chapter Four

# Music for the Alchemist

As we have seen, from very early times, people have believed in the magical properties of gemstones and in the past few decades, 'crystals' as they are now more popularly known, have developed into a multi-million pound/dollar industry. Many gemstones, however, are not what they seem. Many have been ground down and reconstituted; many are even artificially coloured to make them appear more attractive, or to pass themselves off as something they are not. Others are given more glamorous names in an attempt to convince the buyer that the provenance is more impressive than it actually is. And as for the alleged magical attributes ... well, it is extremely difficult to use any rock or mineral as a magical correspondence or amulet if we don't know where it's come from, or to which part of the Earth it relates.

If we are to look at crystals, or more correctly 'minerals', with any real depth of understanding, we need to strip away the veil of fake-lore and superstition, and study them into their correct geological context. Mineralogy is a science largely concerned with the crystalline state of rocks, and in the *Pocket Guide to Minerals*, crystals are defined in the following way:

A crystal is a body bounded by smooth plane surfaces (faces) that are the external expression of an orderly internal atomic arrangement. Minerals, when occurring under conditions favourable to crystal growth, will form well-developed crystals. However, if the growing crystals interfere with one each other they are often poorly formed or distorted. The mineral is still described as crystalline, for no matter how imperfectly formed, it has the same ordered atomic structure and definite chemical composition. Even before the development of the advanced scientific techniques we know today, it was realised that the arrangement of the faces on a crystalline mineral and the angles between these faces were characteristic for that given mineral species. This means that, no matter how poorly formed the crystal is, or of what habit, the angle between the same two faces (if developed) in all crystals of the same mineral species is constant.

**Minerals are now arranged in the internationally used crystallochemical type of classification, which groups together similar types of chemical compounds under the following broad headings. Not all stones and crystals have medicinal or magical powers but by retaining the magic crystals and sacred stones in recognised geological classifications, we can better understand their creation and magical correspondences.**

## Native Elements
**Very few elements occur as minerals in their native state: that is, uncombined with other elements in major proportions.** (*The Illustrated Encyclopaedia of Minerals*)

**Gold:** It was relatively simple for early civilisations to extract gold from the ground, and since it could easily be worked into durable and attractive ornaments, it quickly became recognised as a highly prized possession. Gold is found in many types of rocks but most often in those associated with quartz and pyrites, and because of its bright lustre even when dug straight from the ground, it was magically associated from early times with the Sun and Kingship. In the British Isles, there has been a modest amount of gold mining since early times, especially from the mines in Wales, which provide the gold for Royal wedding rings.

**Silver:** A brilliant, shining white metal that tarnishes quickly to grey or black due to surface oxidation; it often has considerable gold and mercury content (mercury-rich varieties are known amalgam). In ancient times, silver was considered to be worth more than gold because of its rarity; in occultism it is linked with the Moon.

**Copper:** This metal takes its name from the Greek *kypros* for Cyprus and has been beaten into vessels and ornaments for many thousands of years. When mined it is a bright copper-red, tarnishing to a dull brown and often coated with a black or green crust. It is one of the more widely distributed native elements and in occultism is linked with Venus. Copper bracelets are often worn to relieve the pain of arthritis and other ailments.

**Platinum:** The metal did not receive general recognition in ancient times although archaeologists have occasionally uncovered artefacts containing platinum. Large deposits were uncovered during the 16th century Spanish conquest of South America and took its name from the Spanish *Platina del Pinto* after the Rio Pinto, from which its name is taken. Native platinum always contains some iron alloyed with it, and although it is found in igneous rocks associated with olivine, pyroxene, chromite and magnetite, it is usually found as grains or nuggets in river gravels derived from these primary deposits. It has no traditional occult significance.

**Iron:** Native iron occurs very rarely as a terrestrial mineral, except where volcanic rocks cut through coal seams. It is strongly magnetic and forms five per cent of the elements in the Earth's crust; and is thought to be the main component of the Earth's core. It is rarely found in its native state in terrestrial rocks, although it is fairly common in meteorites. In occultism, it is linked to Mars and meteorite iron has had extremely powerful magical associations since Egyptian times.

**Arsenic:** Although white in colour, it quickly tarnishes to dark grey, with a metallic lustre. It is found in close proximity to silver, cobalt and nickel ores in white veins in rock; exhibiting dull, opaque, salt-like crystals. It has a characteristic garlic odour when heated and can be easily confused with native antimony. Extremely toxic, it is used to make insecticides and was a popular medieval poison where the poisoner relied on a course of slow, cumulative dosing to evade detection.

**Antimony:** Similar in appearance to arsenic and associated with silver minerals, stibnite, sphalerite, pyrite and galena. It is a soft, very heavy, bright and metallic mineral, mostly derived from its ore, stibnite. Distinguished from arsenic by the lack of odour when heated, it melts to a metallic globule. Another natural poisonous element, it is used in alloys for making pewter and a pigment for paints and dyes. Medicinally it was formerly used as a purgative; while women in ancient Egypt and Asia once used compounds of antimony in cosmetics.

**Bismuth:** Rare as crystals: silver-white with a reddish hue that darkens with exposure and often an iridescent tarnish will develop. Distinguished from antimony by colour, it is used in medicines, pigments and alloys that melt easily, and although it was known in the Middle Ages, it was not recognised as a distinct element. As a magical correspondence it was associated with Elemental Earth.

**Sulphur** (brimstone): Formed from volcanic gases and found encrusting volcanic vents, fumaroles, and some thermal springs. Bright yellow to yellowish brown with a resinous, greasy lustre, it is most commonly found in sedimentary rocks associated with gypsum and limestone. It is used to make sulphuric acid, matches, insecticides and gunpowder. The stench of sulphur is usually symbolically associated with the Devil and Hell, i.e. 'fire and brimstone' and can be used in ritual magic for magical effect.

**Diamond:** Made from pure carbon and named from the Greek *adamas*, meaning 'invincible' but only around one fifth of the diamonds mined are suitable for use as gemstones, the remainder are used for industrial purposes. Mostly colourless but sometimes pale yellow, blue, green, red or even black — quality gemstones are clear.

As an amulet, the diamond had to be worn on the left arm where they would make the wearer invincible, capable of reconciling quarrels and strife, free from melancholy and madness, and untroubled by nightmares and demons. In occultism, diamonds are associated with 'God', and the emblem of fearlessness and invincibility although many of the references to diamonds in the old lapidaries may have referred to corundum or rock crystal (see Chapter Five).

**Graphite** (plumbago or black lead): Also pure carbon but with a different structure, and although diamonds and graphite are chemically identical, the different atomic arrangements create their dissimilar physical properties. The name graphite is derived from the Greek *graphein*, meaning 'to write' and was coined in 1789 because of its use in making pencils. Black, with a dull metallic or earthy lustre, it is formed by metamorphism of rocks having an appreciable carbon content. It can be found in crystalline limestones, schists, quartzites and metamorphosed coal-beds, but has no known occult significance.

# Key:

**BOLD UPPER CASE** = stones/crystals with some occult, medicinal or historical association.

UPPER CASE = stones/crystals featured in detail elsewhere in the text

The 'crystal craze' has meant that any lump of polished rock can have 'ite' added to its name and be passed off as a genuine mineral. Some stones are ground down, mixed and reconstituted to produce completely bogus minerals for sale, which contain no magical properties or correspondences. *Caveat emptor* — let the buyer beware.

## Sulphides and Sulphosalts

These are chemical compounds in which sulphur is combined with one or more metals *(Pocket Guide to Minerals)*.

Argentite (silver glance): Black with a metallic lustre, crystals frequently occur in groups of parallel growths in large masses in Mexico and Nevada. Found as a primary mineral in association with pyrargyrite, proustite and the most important ore of native silver. **ARGENTITE** is the most important ore of silver and is of great interest to alchemists because it changes its crystal shape at certain temperatures; it is found in veins that have been altered by the action of hot water (hydrothemals) and can be magically associated with Elemental Water.

Arsenopyrite (mispickel): This is an iron arsenide sulphide and the most abundant arsenic mineral, forming under moderately high temperatures, and associated with ores of tin, tungsten, silver and copper. A garlic smell is noted immediately after fracture with a hammer blow. **ARSENOPYRITE** is the most commonplace and widespread ore of arsenic; some specimens are often cross-shaped (cruciform) and could be useful in returning a hex to its originator.

**Bismuthinite** (bismuth glance): Lead-grey to tin-white with an iridescent tarnish. Associated with native bismuth, ARSENOPYRITE, QUARTZ and other sulphides. Usually found in embedded masses with a bladed or fibrous structure, and combined with tin and lead to make low-melting point alloys. BISMUTHINITE is an important component of a wide range of fire safety devices, especially thermally activated fire-detectors. The needle-shaped crystals could be incorporated into an amulet for protection against fire.

**Bornite:** (peacock ore or eruescite from the Latin *erubescere*, meaning 'to turn red'): Common copper mineral, showing copper-red to brown before tarnishing to a characteristic purplish iridescence, hence the name give by old Cornish miners of 'peacock ore' or 'horse-flesh ore'. BORNITE crystals are rare and poor but can be used magically to attune to the powers of Elemental Water, and believed to have the powers of transformation. Also known as PEACOCK ORE when used in raising the Cone of Power for weather control, rain dancing, or harnessing the power of storms.

**Boulangerite:** Bluish lead-grey with a brownish streak. Similar to STIBNITE and jamesonite; x-ray study is often required for positive identification. Found as long prisms and as solid feathering masses, BOULANGERITE could be incorporated into magical charms requiring the metallic element of lead. Magical correspondence: Saturn

**Bournonite** (radelerz or cogwheel ore): Named after the French mineralogist, Count J. L. de Bournon. It is a lead copper antimony sulphide and associated with GALENA, SPHALERITE, CHALCOPYRITE and PYRITE. Highly prized 'cogwheel' specimens were found at the Herodsfoot mine at Liskeard in Cornwall. **BOURNONITE** is steel-grey to black, usually bright on the edges of cogwheel twins, but dull on the broad, flat faces. This striking crystal formation has caught the fancy of miners and collectors the world over, and could be used magically where a dual-gender driving force is needed.

**Chalcopyrite:** Brass-yellow in colour, sometimes with an iridescent tarnish and the primary copper mineral of most porphyry-copper deposits. **CHALCOPYRITE** is also known as 'copper pyrite' and as copper has been widely used by humans since the dawn of the Bronze Age, it can be incorporated into magical working that require the metal as an ingredient. Magical correspondence: Venus

**Chalcosine** (chalcocite or copper glance): Crystals are dark grey to black with a metallic lustre, short prismatic or thick tabular. Most commonly found in the secondary enriched zone of primary copper sulphides, often associated with native copper or cuprite. No known magical correspondences.

**Cinnabar:** This is mercury sulphide, which is the only metal that is liquid at ordinary temperatures. The scarlet red to brownish red colour is its most distinctive feature. **CINNABAR** has been mined since ancient times at Almaden in Spain and was used as vermilion pigment by medieval painters. The name is Persian in origin, meaning 'dragon's blood' and is often found as one of the magical ingredients of spell casting in old *grimories*.

**Cobaltite:** Silver-white to steel-grey, often with a reddish tinge, it is made up of one atom of colbalt, one atom of arsenic and one atom of sulphur. Sometimes alters to pink erythrite (cobalt bloom). **COBALT** gets its name from the German *kobalt*, given to imps that were supposed to live underground and tease the miners. Could be used magically for chthonic-related working.

**Covelline** (covellite): Crystals are rare, usually found in hexagonal plates, mostly massive. Indigo blue (often iridescent) to brass-yellow or purplish-red. **COVELLITE** was first discovered in the 19th century amongst rocks that had been thrown out by Mount Vesuvius — so great was the heat of the eruption that solid covellite was turned into vapour and can therefore be attuned to Elemental Air.

**Enargite:** Found in veins associated with chalcosine, BORNITE, COVELLINE, PYRITE, SPHALERITE, GALENA, BARITE and QUARTZ. Dark grey to black; opaque with a metallic lustre and very rare. No known magical correspondences.

**Galena** (lead glance): Named from the Greek *galena*, meaning 'lead ore', the crystals are usually cubic and lead-grey with a metallic lustre. Associated with a wide variety of other minerals and the most important industrial source of metallic lead, **GALENA** can be associated with the magical correspondences for Saturn and Time.

**Greenockite:** Usually forms as orange-yellow to brick red powdery coating to zinc minerals such as SPHALERITE. It is named in honour of Lord Greenock, a 19th century British soldier, but has no known magical correspondences.

**Jamesonite:** Fibrous crystals together with massive columns, this is grey-black, sometimes with an iridescent tarnish associated with other sulphides and sulpho-salts. Crystals are not flexible like those of stibnite. Sometimes known as 'grey antimony', it has no known magical correspondences.

**Marcasite:** Pale bronze-yellow with a metallic lustre, it occurs most often in near-surface deposits. **MARCASITE** is often used for jewellery but no known traditional occult significance, although it could be used for casting deception.

**Millerite**: Brass–yellow fine needles often in radiating groups, frequently as tufts of slender crystals in cavities in limestone or dolomite, often as an alteration product of other nickel-rich minerals. Sometimes found in meteorites, **MILLERITE** is in great demand with collectors, partly because of its great beauty and partly because of its scarcity. A geode with millerite on quartz would make an excellent focus for cosmic meditation.

**Molybdenite:** Used to produce very tough machine-toll metals with tungsten, as an alloy in steel. Lead-grey, sometimes with bluish tinges, it is found as an accessory mineral in some granites. No known magical correspondences.

**Nickeline** (niccolite): Occurs rarely as pyramidal crystals of pale copper-red, often altering on surfaces to pale green annabergite (nickel bloom). Found with pyrrhotine, CHALCOPYRITE and other nickel sulphides in basic igneous rocks. No known magical correspondences.

**Orpiment:** Rarely occurs as short prismatic crystals; usually as foliated or granular masses associated with REALGAR. A major ore of arsenic. **ORPIMENT** is lemon-yellow to brownish-yellow, transparent to translucent, with a resinous, pearly lustre and used as an artist's pigment. Medieval alchemists used to combine it with copper to produce a mixture than resembled gold in colour.

**Pentlandite:** A bronze-yellow mineral and one of the most important ores of nickel. Usually found in igneous rocks with iron and nickel sulphides and arsenides, accumulated by magmatic segregation, and intergrown with pyrrhotine. **PENTLANDITE** is the world's principal source of nickel; it is also found in meteorites and could be incorporated into magical workings that require a degree of magnetic (drawing or repelling) energy.

**Pyrargyrite:** Usually in hexagonal prisms with pyramidal terminations: twinning is common, forming 'swallow-tail' groups. Deep red that darkens on exposure. Pyrargyrite and proustite are commonly called 'ruby sheer ores', although the latter is rarer. Associated with native silver, ARGENTINE, tetrahedrite, GALENA and SPHALERITE. No known magical correspondences.

**Pyrite** (iron pyrites or fool's gold): Takes its name from the Greek *pyrites lithos*, meaning 'stone which strikes fire', referring to its habit of sparking when struck by iron. Crystals are commonly cubic; fossils are often replaced by pyrite. Pale brass-yellow, pyrite is one of the most widely distributed sulphide minerals. The lack of tarnish in **PYRITE** earned it the name of 'fool's gold'. Sometimes used as amulets by Native Americans, and 'the belief in the magic power is attested by their presence among the various objects that medicine men use in the course of their incantations'.

## Fool's Gold

Pyrite is also known as **HAEPHESTITE**, named for the Greek god of fire, Haephaestos, the stone calmed civil uprisings, hurricanes and hailstones, kept locusts and blight from ripening crops, and preserved its owner from all danger. A brilliant stone, "it darted forth fiery, golden rays, and had to be worn either on the left arm, or over the heart to work at its best" (*Magical Jewels*). The stone is described as being fully capable of burning the hand that clutches it ... "on weathering, pyrite does produce sulphuric acid and if grasped by a hand that is moist from perspiration, it *can* chemically react by burning the hand" (*A Field Guide to Rocks & Minerals*). Magically it is also used for casting deception, where all is not as it first seems — or to see through the deception of others. Use for deception and covering tracks.

**Pyrrhotine** (pyrrhotite or magnetic pyrites): Occasionally found as rosettes of hexagonal platy crystals, bronze-yellow tarnishing to brown. Occurs principally in basic igneous rocks. Its name derives from the Greek word *pur*, meaning 'fire' but it has no known magical correspondences other than being attuned to Elemental Fire.

**Realgar:** An arsenic sulphide taking its name from the Arabic *rahj al ghar*, meaning 'powder of the mine' alluding to its bright orange colour. Specimens should be kept in darkened containers as the mineral disintegrates on exposure to light. **REALGAR** is still sometimes used as an artist's pigment despite the risk of poisoning.

**Skutterudite, Smaltite and Chloanthite Series:** Three minerals with similar properties. Tin-white to silver-grey, with an iridescent or greyish tarnish; associated with COBALTITE, nickeline, ARSENOPYRITE, silver and bismuth. No known magical correspondences.

**Sphalerite** (blende): Named from the Greek *sphaleros*, meaning 'deceitful', which refers to its tendency to occur in a number of forms that can easily be mistaken for other minerals. It is the most common zinc mineral and is associated with GALENA, CHALCOPYRIE and PYRITE; yellow, brown to black with increasing iron content. The black variety of **SPHALERITE** is known as 'Black Jack' and could possibly be used in charms requiring an element of deceit.

**Stibnite** (antimony glance): Found in association with quartz, REALGAR, ORPIMENT, CINNABAR, SPHALERITE, BARITE and GALENA. A spectacular mineral that can produce magnificent prisms and blades reaching up to 60cm in length. Blackish-grey with an iridescent tarnish and the most common antimony mineral. Used in the commercial manufacture of matches and fireworks, **STIBNITE** could be associated with Elemental Fire.

**Tetrahedrite** and **Tennantite**: Dark grey to black with a metallic lustre they are found in veins associated with copper, lead, silver and zinc minerals — although tennantite is less common. No known magical correspondences.

**Wurtzite:** Found in pyramid-shaped crystals; brownish-black, opaque to translucent. Rather rare, it is usually found in sulphide ores formed from acidic fluids. No known magical correspondences.

## Oxides

**There are over 150 oxide minerals known but relatively few provide attractive specimens** (*The Illustrated Encyclopaedia of Minerals*).

**Anatase** (octahedrite): Comes in various shades of yellow and brown, deep blue or black, transparent to nearly opaque. Occurs as an accessory mineral in igneous and metamorphic rocks. Commonly associated with QUARTZ, brookite and RUTILE but there are no known magical correspondences.

**Bauxite:** The name given to deposits rich in hydrous aluminium oxides. It is mostly a mixture of gibbsite, boehmite and diaspore. Formed by prolonged tropical weathering and leaching of silica from rocks containing aluminium silicates and is the only important source of aluminium. Gibbsite (hydrargillite) is white, grey or sometimes pink or red, and translucent to transparent. **BAUXITE** is the world's most important source of the valuable metallic element aluminium; it could be used in magical working that requires lightness and strength, i.e. 'an iron fist in a velvet glove'.

**Braunite:** A brownish-black to steel-grey mineral with a submetallic lustre, often found in hydrothermal veins with other manganese oxides, also formed as the product of metamorphism of manganese bearing sediments. No known magical correspondences.

**Brookite:** An accessory mineral in igneous and metamorphic rocks, it is reddish-brown to brownish-black in colour. No known magical correspondences.

**Brucite:** A white to pale green or blue mineral, translucent to transparent, it is found in metamorphosed dolomitic limestones and in veins of SERPENTINE. Usually associated with CALCITE, ARAGONITE, TALC and MAGNETITE, **BRUCITE** is impossible to melt and could therefore be magically associated with protection against fire.

**Cassiterite:** Named from the Greek *kassiteros*, meaning 'tin', it is usually found in massive forms of prisms and pyramids. This is one of the few tin minerals and almost the sole source of the metal; fine crystalline specimens come from a number of localities in Cornwall. **CASSITERITE**, which was formerly called 'tinstone' in English, has been known to man since the Bronze Age. The ancient Greeks called their main source 'the Cassiterite Islands' and although no one knows the exact location of these islands, it may be a reference to ancient Britain.

**Chromite:** A member of the SPINEL group, it is of great importance in the manufacture of stainless steel. Found as an accessory mineral in igneous rocks such as periodtite and SERPENTINE, chromite is the only natural source of the metallic element chromium. No known magical correspondences.

**Chrysoberyl** (alexandrite): **CHRYSOBERYL** is possibly the most interesting of all gemstones and highly popular in 17th and 18th century Europe for jewellery, especially in Spain and Portugal. The rare **ALEXANDRITE** variety, because of its absorption of light in the critical yellow-green part of the spectrum, appears green by daylight and purple or red by artificial light. The discovery of this variety in 1831 coincided with the day Alexander II of Russia (then heir-apparent) reached his majority. Looked upon as a stone of good omen in Russia, it balances the emotions, and used magically to aid Otherworld experiences, especially as it is now manufactured synthetically at great cost for use in the windows of spacecraft, because it can filter out harmful cosmic rays! **CYMOPHANE** is the scientific name for the valuable cat's eye variety of chrysoberyl, which is used as a charm against evil spirits. The only other minerals and gemstones that show the cat's eye optical effect are APATITE, CHATOYANT QUARTZ, SCAPOLITE and TOURMALINE.

**Corundum** (ruby and sapphire): The name is believed to derive from the Sanskrit *kuruvinda*, meaning 'ruby' and next to the diamond is the hardest mineral. The transparent red-coloured variety is ruby — the colour is thought to be due to the presence of a little vanadium; the blue gem variety, sapphire, is coloured by a little iron or titanium. The **SAPPHIRE** was said to cure melancholy, release the mind from care, and mended manners. **Medical:** It cured sore eyes, dysentery, heart disease, skin ailments, bruises and inflammations and, being an emblem of chastity, was often set in rings to be worn by the clergy. It also strengthened the intellect of its owner and to grant a superior degree of understanding. When worn often and consistently it eliminated stupidity, and calmed obstinate and unruly passions but the effects only lasted for as long as the stone was worn. **Magical:** The stone is a powerful defence from harm and preserves the wearer from envy, and attracts divine favour (see STAR SAPPHIRE — Chapter Ten). The glowing hue of the **RUBY** suggested the idea that an inextinguishable flame burned inside the stone. **Medical:** The ruby drove away sleep and also harmed the brain, although it also dispels disorientated, trapped energy. **Magical:** There are many talismanic virtues attributed to the stone and all the good effects "were most surely secured if the ruby, set in a ring, bracelet or brooch, were worn on the left side" (*Magical Jewels*) (see STAR RUBY — Chapter Ten). The transparent or translucent **CORUNDUM** (adamant or adamas) resembles many silicate minerals and is harder than any other natural mineral except diamond for which it may have been mistaken in many classic translations. **Medical:** Has all the same properties as a diamond, with which it was often confused in translations of ancient manuscripts. **Magical:** The magical virtues brings victory, averts evil dreams, poison and strife

**Cuprite:** A secondary mineral, usually forming at or near the Earth's surface by the oxidation of copper sulphide veins, and usually associated with other secondary copper minerals such as MALACHITE, AZURITE and native copper. **CUPRITE** crystals are dark red, sometimes nearly black, and some fine specimens have come from Redruth and Liskeard in Cornwall. Magical correspondence: Venus

**Franklinite:** A member of the SPINEL group, this is opaque black with reddish-brown to dark-brown streaks. Franklinite, ZINCITE and willemite occur together in the zinc deposits of Franklin, New Jersey. The deposits are associated with crystalline limestone and are probably of a metasomatic origin, i.e.

metamorphic change that involves the introduction of material from an external source. No known magical correspondences.

**Geothite:** Named after the German author and scientist, J. W. von Goethe, although fine stalactite specimens occur in several localities in Cornwall; also found in bogs and lagoons. It is yellowish brown to dark brown in colour, with a yellowish brown streak. Limonite is an impure hydrated iron oxide largely composed of goethite, found mainly as weathered crusts or as bog or marine deposits. **GEOTHITE** is often mined for its high iron content (which aligns it magically with Mars and strength), and used by artists as a yellow pigment.

**Haematite** (kidney ore): Named from the Greek *haima*, meaning 'blood' because many of the specimens are red coloured and all have a red streak. This is the most important ore of iron and widely distributed. Fine specimens can be found in Cumbria. Specularite is the popular name for crystallised haematite in the form of brilliant blue-black crystals. **HAEMATITE** was used as an important red pigment in medieval frescoes and manuscripts. **Medicinal:** Because of its associations with iron and blood, this is a stone of Mars. Used as a talisman it procurers a 'fortunate issue of law suits and judgements'. **Magical:** Used for creating bursts of psychic energy, releasing magical powers and successfully concluding magical workings. Brings freedom from restrictions and grounds disruptive or negative energies. **ILMENITE:** A widely distributed as an accessory mineral in igneous rocks, it is named after the location in the Ilmen Mountains in the USSR where it was first discovered. The mineral is an important source of the metal titanium but has no known magical correspondences.

**Lepidocrocite:** Red to brown with a dull orange streak, it is usually found as a secondary mineral associated with

GEOTHITE. No known magical correspondences.

**Magnetite:** An iron oxide named for its strong magnetic properties and like HEMATITE is a major industrial source of metallic iron. Commonly found as an accessory mineral in igneous rocks and as magmatic segregation deposits; also as a detrital mineral in beach or river sands where it can be extracted with a magnet. **MAGNETITE** is used in crystal healing to 'draw out' pain and disease, or to release mental and emotional blockages and encourage psychic energy to flow again. Magically it is known as **LODESTONE** and used to increase power within a magical working. Some esoteric sources say they should be used in pairs to gain full benefit (one to attract positive elements and the other to repel negative elements). Gives strength and courage.

## A Lodestone Amulet

Loadstone or magnetite amulet, when worn around the neck aids the memory and is used as a test for truth or faithfulness. The lodestone enables the bearer to foretell the future and will endow them with divine inspiration and secret knowledge. If a question is asked about the future, it will reveal a truthful answer.

To make an amulet you will need about 10 inches of 18-guage silver wire to wrap around the stone just as you would wrap a parcel — from side to side and from top to bottom. When you are sure the stone cannot fall out, create a loop at the top by winding the wire around a thin pencil. Weave the wire back through the cage and when it is secure, remove the pencil, leaving the loop open enough to thread through a key ring, piece of cord or neck chain — or placed in a small pouch to be carried around in a handbag or briefcase.

*How to Make Amulets, Charms & Talismans*, Deborah Lippman and Paul Colin

**Manganite:** A prismatic black crystal associated with granite rocks and deposited in bogs, lakes and shallow marine environments. Often found associated with pyrolusite, GEOTHITE and BARYTE, **MANGANITE** is one of the most important sources of manganese, a metal widely used in the manufacture of steel, which could be incorporated into a charm for strength.

**Psilomelane:** A name now applied to the mineral in which barium is an important constituent. Consecretionary forms are common in lake and swamp deposits. No known magical correspondences.

**Pyrochlore** and **Microlite:** Usually associated with alkaline igneous rocks with ZIRCON and APATITE, tantalite and columbite. Some species are radioactive due to uranium and thorium. No known magical correspondences.

**Pyrolusite:** A delicate, dark-grey formation that appears like a fossilised leaf. It is a secondary mineral formed by the oxidation of manganite and other primary manganese minerals. Historically, it was used to remove unwanted green and brown impurities from clear glass, with earned it the name of 'glass-maker's soap'. No known magical correspondences.

**Rutile:** Named for the Latin *rutilis*, meaning 'red glowing', although some of the specimens may be nearly black. Together with ilenite and sphene, **RUTILE** is a source of titanium; it commonly occurs as needle-like inclusions in quartz crystals, where it has the effect of needles and thread frozen into a ball of ice. Widespread accessory mineral in igneous rocks. Often the clear rock crystal selected for scrying is shot through with rutile and known as **RUTILATED QUARTZ**.

**Spinel:** A metamorphic mineral found in crystalline limestones and schists, this beautifully coloured gemstone is frequently found in stream sands but in its purest form it is colourless. Many of the stones from Sri Lanka are dull blue, greenish blue and purple in colour, caused by iron; other colours are red (ruby spinel), grey (gahnite), green (hercynite) and red-brown (galaxite). The colour of **RUBY SPINEL** derives from the Italian *spinella*, meaning 'little thorns' in reference to one of the typical crystal shapes. Large ruby spinel crystals are found in the crown jewels of the world and despite their names, the so-called Timor Ruby and the Black Prince's Ruby in the British crown jewels are in fact not rubies at all but ruby spinels. The crown jewels of the former Shahs of Iran contain two large ruby spinels and the world's most beautiful ruby spinel is thought to be the 400-carat specimen in the crown jewels of Russia.

**Tungstite** (tungsten ochre): Usually formed by the oxidation of wolframite and is found associated with it in tungsten deposits. Yellow to yellowish-green, translucent with a resinous lustre. No known magical correspondences.

**Uraninite** (pitchblende): A dramatic mineral that is black with bright yellow or green alteration patches and the chief ore of the radioactive element uranium. Crystalline uraninite is associated with ZIRCON, TOURMALINE, monazite, mica and FELDSPAR. Highly radioactive and the chief industrial source of uranium, it has no known magical correspondences apart from destruction and weaponry.

**Zincite:** A very rare but beautiful mineral, found in few localities where it occurs in association with CALCITE, franklinite and willemite. The basic colour is orange-yellow but some specimens contain impurities of manganese, which cause them to take on a distinctive red tone. The most spectacular pieces are not natural minerals, but occurring during zinc-smelting processes in the old-type furnaces of Eastern Europe. **ZINCITE** is worn to increase vitality, enhance creativity and personal power.

## Zincite amulet

These crystals are beautiful and rare, and consequently highly valued. Although they may be cut into a wide range of decorative shapes, they are usually too fragile to withstand wear and tear. Keep the gemstone in a tiny pouch and wear it around the neck for the best results. Magically, zincite is used as a pick-me-up when extra boosts of energy are needed to increase vitality, enhance creativity to fulfil an important project, or attract personal power. The gem should only be worn or carried for limited periods as the prolonged energy boost can also be extremely debilitating.

## Halides

**These are compounds containing one of the halogen elements (chlorine, fluorine, bromine, etc). The best known minerals are halite and fluorite.** *(The Illustrated Encyclopaedia of Minerals)*

**Atacamite:** Commonly found as bright green to dark green slender, prismatic crystals, this is a secondary mineral in the oxidised zone of copper deposits, especially in arid saline conditions. Often associated with MALACHITE, CUPRITE, CHRYSO-COLLA, brochantite, GYPSUM and limonite. No known magical correspondences.

**Carnallite:** Colourless to white but sometimes red-orange due to minute HEMATITE inclusions. Found in the upper layers of evaporite deposits together with HALITE and SYLVINE. Mined and used as a source of potassium for fertilisers. No known magical correspondences.

**Chlorargyrite** (horn silver or cerargyrite): Colourless when fresh but becoming violet-brown on exposure to light; secondary mineral occurring in the oxidised zones of silver deposits, especially in arid regions. Commonly associated with native silver, CERUSSITE and limonite. No known magical correspondences.

**Cryolite:** Found in major quantities but only at a few locations worldwide. Associated with microcline, QUARTZ, SIDERITE, GALENA and FLUORITE and used to make enamels and glass. **CRYOLITE** crystals are almost invisible in water and resemble blocks of ice; the name is derived from the Greek word *kruos*, meaning 'icy-cold'. Could be used in charms for 'freezing someone out'.

**Fluorite** (fluorspar): Named from the Latin *fluere*, meaning 'to flow', and referring to the ease with which it melts, this is one of the most beautiful of crystals, forming in many different colours from yellow and green to violet, although it is colourless and transparent when pure. The phenomenon of it being able to emit visible light on exposure to ultra-violet beams, gave us the term 'fluorescence'. Beautiful specimens of **FLORITE** have been found in Derbyshire, Cumbria and Co. Durham and the purple-banded variety exclusively from Castleton in Derbyshire, popularly known as **BLUE JOHN**, is highly sought after for ornamental work but is too soft for use in jewellery. The first occurrence of this name is recorded in *The Oxford English Dictionary* dated 1772, but the mineral itself is known to have been extracted from the Earth since ancient times. Magically it is said to encourage creativity and lessen the fear of failure; should be carried on any magical quest or spiritual path.

**Halite** (rock salt): Better known as sodium chloride, with its name deriving from the Greek *hals*, meaning 'salt'. Halite is one of the few important minerals that are readily soluble in water. It is widespread in large saline sedimentary deposits, where it has formed by the evaporation of seawater. **SALT** is obtained commercially either by mining these deposits or by natural evaporation of brine in shallow ponds and has numerous uses in medicine and magic.

**Mendipite** and **Chloroxiphite**: The former is found in the manganese deposits of the Mendip Hills (Somerset); the latter is a rare secondary mineral associated with mendipite. No known magical correspondences.

**Sylvine**: Found in bedded salt deposits and associated with, but less common that HALITE because of its greater solubility in water. Also found as encrustations in volcanic fumaroles especially at Mount Vesuvius, where it was first discovered in 1823. **SYLVINE** is named after Franz Sylvius, a German anatomist and chemist who prescribed a potion known as *sal digestive Sylvii* derived from the mineral to cure excess stomach acid.

## Salt

For all its commonplaces uses, salt is one of the most magical of Earth's minerals. It is the symbol of incorruptibility and therefore eternity; in magical terms salt is considered a powerful defensive weapon against the powers of evil. It is erroneously stated in many texts that witches cannot eat food that contains salt, since it features strongly in many traditional Craft applications. It also has alchemical associations with mercury and sulphur, and the Empress card of the Tarot. To eat salt under someone's roof creates a sacred bond between host and guest: no one who has eaten of another's salt should speak ill of him, or do him an ill turn. (*The Dictionary of Mystery & Magic*, Melusine Draco)

# Carbonates

**Although over 70 carbonate mineral species are known, three of them, calcite, dolomite and siderite, account for the majority of the carbonate material in the Earth's crust.** *(The Illustrated Encyclopaedia of Minerals)*

**Ankerite:** Similar to DOLOMITE, this is found in sulphide veins especially associated with iron ores, and frequently fills joints in coal seams. No known magical correspondences.

**Aragonite:** It received its name from the Aragon district of Spain where the mineral occurs. It forms the main component of the shells of many organisms, such as corals and oysters and a coral-like form, known as *flos-feri* (iron flower) is sometimes found in the iron mines of Austria. **ARAGONITE** is used as a comforter or 'worry stone' to help relieve stress and tension. Also used magically to encourage mental ability and quicken the wits. Associated with Elemental Water.

**Aurichalcite:** A pretty blue-green hued crystal with a silky to pearl lustre, it is widespread as a secondary mineral in the oxidised zones of zinc-copper deposits. No known magical correspondences.

**Azurite** (chessylite): Azure blue in colour, this is found as a secondary copper mineral, often inter-banded with MALACHITE; also associated with CHRYSOCOLLA, chalcosine, CALCITE, limonite and other secondary copper minerals. **AZURITE** was often cut and mounted as a cabochon gem; and a major source of blue pigment used by painters in the Middle Ages. Magically it is used to wear down the opposition, conceal magical activities and develop psychic powers. Often found with malachite, these two stones will often enhance each other when combined with a view to developing those psychic powers.

**Calcite:** Named from the Greek *chalx*, meaning 'burnt lime'. It is a very common material, found in many different environments. It is the major component of several calcareous sedimentary rocks, such as limestone and chalk, and of metamorphic rock marble. It may form by the direct precipitation from seawater, or by the accumulation of shell material on the sea floor. Stalactites and stalagmites are often formed by the re-desposition of calcium carbonate and the **CALCITE** or **ICELAND SPAR** (also called Iceland crystal) demonstrate the optical property of 'double refraction' — light passing through is split into two components, giving a double image of any object viewed through them. Perfect for scrying and divination, encourages spontaneity and creativity, and opens the doors of opportunity

**Cerussite:** Named from the Latin *cerussa*, meaning a white lead pigment. Next to GALENA, this is the most common ore of lead; occurring in lead veins, associated with galena and anglesite, it is formed by the action of carbonated water on these minerals. The crystals often form exquisite 'leaf' formations and occur as a common secondary mineral found in the oxidised zone of ore deposits containing galena. **CERUSSITE** can be associated with Elemental Water for meditational purposes.

**Dolomite:** Named after D de Dolomieu, a French mineralogist, who first noticed the difference between CALCITE and dolomite — a rock-forming mineral in the tremendous masses of dolomitic limestones and dolomitic marbles. **DOLOMITE** can be both a mineral and a rock, the most famous form being the marble that comes from Carrara in Tuscany. It is also a source of magnesium and many magnesium compounds are used as purgatives in medicine.

**Leadhillite:** Found in the oxidised zone of lead deposits as a secondary mineral associated with CERUSSITE, anglestite, lanarkite, linarite, pyromorphite and GALENA. No known magical correspondences.

**Magnesite:** Formed by the alteration of rocks consisting largely of magnesium silicates and by waters rich in carbonate. Found in stratiform beds of metamorphic origin with talc-chlorie or mica-schists, also as a replacement of calchite rocks by magnesium bearing solutions. **MAGNESITE** is one of the most valuable minerals known and important in medicine, where it is a source of the purgative Epsom salts and various laxatives.

**Malachite:** Named form the Greek *malache*, meaning 'mallow' in reference to its green leaf colour, and is found in deposits in which copper sulphides are available for alteration. **MALACHITE** was used as a bright green pigment on medieval panel paintings and manuscripts, it is now more likely to be used in the manufacture of small, decorative objects, although larger slabs of it decorate some of the halls of the Winter Palace in Leningrad, and the columns of St Isaac's cathedral. **Medical:** Helps free the wearer from old life patterns and unreasonable relationships. **Magical:** Used for its ability to turn aside or reduce magical or mental attacks (see **Azurite**), particularly against children. Engraved with the image of the Sun, this became a powerful talisman and protects the wearer from enchantments, evil spirits, and the attacks of venomous creatures.

**Rhodochrosite:** Named from the Greek *rhodokhros*, meaning 'of rosy colour', in allusion to its unusual colour. **RHODOCHRISITE** is often found in veins carrying silver, lead and copper ores and is believed to encourage creativity, be a bringer of joy and relieve inner turmoil. Brings freedom from entrapment and oppressive situations. Banded specimens from Argentina are sometimes marketed under the name of **INCA ROSE.**

**Siderite** (chalybite): Named from the Greek *sideros*, meaning 'iron', this is widespread as bedded deposits or flaky clusters in sedimentary rocks, and is a major source of iron. The alternative name chalybite (from the Greek *chalyps*, meaning 'steel') is rarely used. This is unfortunate because 'siderite' has three other connotations: it is an alternative name for hornblende and lazulite, and also a term used to describe iron meteorites. The mineral **SIDERITE** is formed exclusively beneath the surface of the Earth and has no extraterrestrial sources; it could however be identified with the magical correspondence for Mars.

**Smithsonite** (calamine): Named after the founder of the Smithsonian Institute, James Smithson, this mineral can be found in the oxidised zones of most zinc-ore deposits in a wide variety of colours. No known magical correspondences.

**Witherite:** Associated with BARITE and GALENA, the crystals are always twinned, creating 'pseudo' hexagonal forms. Powdered witherite will colour a flame apple-green (arium), readily distinguishing the mineral from strontianite (red). Strontianite is often associated with celestite, BARITE and calcite. **CELESTITE** is used to bring order to chaos and aids astral working — its name means 'stone of heaven'.

## A Malachite and Azurite Neck Pouch

Often found together, these two stones will often enhance each other when combined with a view to developing psychic powers. A gem pouch can be a special form of magical working, and carrying the gemstones with you in a neck-pouch is an easy way of making use of their powers. If purchasing the stones from a shop or via mail order they will need to be psychically cleansed before using. The pouch should be of white or silver fabric, or soft white leather. "Into the pouch put the pieces of azurite and malachite and pass through the smoke of patchouli joss or incense; put the pouch on immediately and perform some simple psychic exercise — showing the pouch what you expect it to do" *The Gemstones Handbook*, Christine Sempers.

## Sulphates

**There are many sulphate minerals but only a few are common enough to provide good specimens.** *(The Pocket Guide to Minerals)*

**Alunite:** Small, rare crystals usually found as near-surface rocks of volcanic regions, which have been altered by solutions bearing sulphuric acid. **ALUNITE** is an important source of potash alum, which is used to make dyes and pigments; and in medicine as an astringent or styptic to contract blood vessels and stem bleeding.

**Anglesite:** A lead sulphate deriving its name from the Welsh island of Anglesey and is similar structure of BARYTE and CELESTINE. Small fragments of **ANGLESITE** will fuse in a candle flame and can be used for a binding or bringing-together ritual.

**Baryte** (barites or barite): The name comes from the Greek *barys*, meaning 'heavy'. The crystals are sometimes tinged yellow, blue or brown; in some specimens the crystals form spectacular growths known as cockscomb masses. It is a common mineral in lead and zinc veins, where it occurs in association with GALENA, SPHALERITE, FLOURITE and QUARTZ. Some specimens are fluorescent and phosphorescent in ultraviolet light; as powder, it will colour a flame apple-green (barium). **SEPTARIAN** nodules of barite found in the 'bad lands' of South Dakota contain up to four-inch fluorescent, transparent amber-coloured crystals; used shamanically it is a stone of deep and ancient wisdom, and moving between the worlds. The flower-like **DESERT ROSE** is said to add great power to any magical working, breaking down barriers, and increasing confidence.

**Brochantite:** Commonly forms as dusty crusts and aggregates of crystals as a secondary mineral in the oxidised zone of copper deposits, especially in arid regions. No known magical correspondences.

**Celestine** (celestite): The name comes from the Latin *caelestis*, meaning 'of the sky', referring to the blue hue of many specimens. It occurs as a sedimentary deposit associated with HALITE, GYPSUM and clay. Colours a flame crimson (strontium). **CELESTINE** is often used for the purposes of inducing lucid dreaming and can be associated with Elemental Air, as it is used in the manufacture of distress flares and other pyrotechnics.

**Crocoite:** A dramatic confusion of bright orange to red crystals, this rare secondary mineral is found in the oxidised zone of lead-chromium veins, together with other secondary lead minerals such as CERUSSITE and pyromorphite. This delicate and rare mineral, **CROCOITE** provided artists with a completely new shade of orange.

**Epsomite** (Epsom salt): Named after the English town where the mineral occurs in mineral springs, and where it was first discovered in 1695. It is also found as encrusting masses on the walls of caves and mine workings where rocks rich in magnesium have been exposed. Also formed from some mineral waters and in volcanic fumaroles. **EPSOMITE** has a great range of uses in medicine and pharmaceuticals. It is also an important product in veterinary medicine, particularly in the treatment of local inflammations and infected wounds.

**Gypsum:** The name comes from the Greek *gupsos*, meaning

'chalk, plaster or cement'. It is most commonly found as a saline residue resulting from the evaporation of enclosed basins of seawater, especially in the Triassic rocks of England and Wales. Anhydrite is an important rock-forming mineral, found in bedded evaporite deposits, and may be deposited directly from seawater or formed by the dehydration of gypsum. **GYPSUM** and anhydrite are both forms of calcium sulphate, but gypsum contains water in its structure and is a much more common mineral. Another form of gypsum with a use that can be traced back to ancient times, is the semi-transparent **ALABASTER**; this variety can be artificially coloured and is often passed off as jade. Mounted in brass this stone is given as a good luck charm, especially if egg-shaped; it possesses qualities of protection and brings good fortune.

**Jarosite:** Found as crusts or coatings on and associated with iron ores. Plumbojarosite forms as minute tabular crystals as a secondary mineral found in oxidised zones of lead deposits. No known magical correspondences.

**Linarite:** Deep blue and translucent, this is a rare but distinctive secondary mineral found in the oxidised zone of some lead-copper ores. **LINARITE** forms in parts of the Earth where lead and copper veins have been altered by circulating fluid, mainly water, and could be identified with Elemental Water. Linarite crystals are prismatic and often appear jumbled up together in strikingly unusual formations.

**Scheelite:** Often accompanies wolframite and will fluoresce under ultraviolet light. Associated with cassiterite, molybdenite, FLOURITE and TOPAZ. Also found in some contact metamorphic deposits with garnet, axinite, idocrase and wollastonite. No known magical correspondences.

**Wolframite:** Found in quartz veins associated with metallic ores and can be weakly magnetic. No known magical correspondences.

**Wulfenite:** Brilliant crystals form in square tabular plates, sometimes very thin, short prismatic or stubby. Found as a secondary mineral formed in the oxidised deposits of lead and molybdenum minerals, commonly associated with vanadinite, CERUSSITE, ANGLESITE and pyromorphite. No known magical correspondences.

## Lucid Dreaming using Celestine

This is a half-waking, half-dream state where the magical practitioner is fully conscious and aware of his/her surroundings, but still able to receive images or impressions from the astral. The astral image is often superimposed over the immediate surroundings like the double-exposure on a photograph. For psychic answers to personal questions, hold a piece of celestine between the palms of the hand, and gaze into a candle flame placed just below eye level. Concentrate on the question in mind and hold the concentration for as long as possible ... gradually images will begin to move on the periphery of your vision that will stimulate answers.

## Phosphates & Arsenates

**The phosphates form a large group of minerals but most of them are rare and only form inconspicuous crystals.** *(The Illustrated Encyclopaedia of Minerals)*

**Adamite:** Crystals usually small and merged together in crusts. Copper-bearing varieties are shades of green, cobalt-bearing varieties are violet-rose, more commonly yellowish-green. A secondary mineral found in the oxidised zone of ore deposits containing primary zinc and arsenic-rich mineral. Often encrusting limonite. Some **ADAMITE** specimens fluoresce lemon-yellow in ultraviolet light and are highly sought after by mineral collectors. Can be aligned with the planetary association of Venus.

**Amblygonite:** White to creamy white; also pale shades of green, blue, pink or yellow, it is found in granite and other lithium and phosphate-rich minerals. **AMBLYGONITE** is extremely rare and gem-quality specimens are highly valued by collectors. It occurs only in granite pegmatities, igneous rocks that formed originally through volcanic activity deep beneath the surface of the Earth — and so can be attuned to Elemental Earth. The world's largest faceted gem came originally from Brazil and can now be seen in the mineralogical collection at the Smithsonian Institute in Washington, USA.

**Apatite:** The name derives from the Greek *apate*, meaning 'deceit', owing to its misleading similarity to other minerals. The crystals are sometimes cut as gemstones for collectors and the mineral is the principal component of human bones and teeth. Because **APATITE** can take on a wide range of shapes and colours, it has often been mistaken for other minerals, particularly BERYL, OLIVINE, QUARTZ and TOURMALINE. In all these cases, however, the key test is hardness — apatite is softer than nearly all the materials it resembles. Could be used magically in rituals of deception.

**Brazilianite**: One of the most recently discovered gemstones unearthed in 1944 in pegmatite deposits in Brazil. Pegmatities are coarse-grained rocks that were originally formed through volcanic activity. Seldom found in jeweller's shops, it is greatly prized by mineral collectors; a yellow stone often mistaken for yellow CHRYSOBERYL, BERYL and TOPAZ. No known magical correspondences.

**Chalcopyhyllite:** The emerald green or bluish-green crystals are thin tabular, six-sided forms, also foliated masses or rosettes. This is a rare secondary mineral in the oxidised zone of copper-bearing ore deposits associated with other copper minerals. Its name — **CHALCOPYHYLLITE** is derived from the Greek words *chalkos,* meaning 'copper', and *phyllon,* meaning 'leaf' — referring to the mineral's main metal and its characteristically foliated crystals. Could be associated magically with Venus.

**Childrenite:** A rare mineral, but sometimes found as fine crystals in some hydrothermal vein deposits. No known magical correspondences.

**Erythrite** (cobalt bloom) and **Annabergite** (nickel bloom): Cobalt and nickel substitute for one another to form a complete composition series. Erythrite is crimson-red and pink' with magnificent needle-shaped crystals. Annabergite is apple-green — both are secondary minerals produced by the surface oxidisation of COBALT and nickel arsenides in some ore deposits. No known magical correspondences.

**Lazulite:** Deep azure blue (also paler shades of blue) this is a rare mineral found in some metamorphic rocks as grains or masses, especially in quartzites. Found associated with high-grade metamorphic minerals such as kyanite, sillimanite, CORUNDUM, muscovite and GARNET. No known magical correspondences.

**Libethenite:** A secondary mineral found in the oxidised zone of copper ore deposits, associated with other primary and secondary copper minerals. Its shiny dark green crystals can be easily confused with OLIVENITE. **LIBETHENITE** could be assigned magically to Venus as the colour green and copper are the correct correspondences.

**Liroconite:** Sky-blue to green in thin, wedge-shaped crystals. A rare secondary mineral found in the oxidised zone of copper deposits associated with AZURITE, MALACHITE, cuprite, oliveniye, chalcophyllite and limonite. Its name is derived from the Greek words for 'pale' and 'powder'. No known magical correspondences.

**Ludlamite:** Bright to apple green crystals occurring as a secondary mineral in the oxidisation zone of ore deposits and as an alteration product of primary iron phosphate minerals — often associated with vivianite. No known magical correspondences.

**Monazite:** Found as an accessory mineral in granitic and associated rocks; also in gneissic metamorphic rocks. Detrital sands derived from those rocks often contain considerable commercial quantities of monozite. **MONAZITE** is used to make components in cigarette lighters and nuclear power plants — and can therefore be associated with both Elemental Air and Elemental Fire!

**Pyromorphite** and **Mimetite** form a series of minerals in which phosphorus and arsenic replace one another. The name pyromorphite derives from the Greek *pyr*, meaning 'fire' and morphe, meaning 'form' referring to it property of taking up a crystalline form after heating; mimetes, 'an imitator', refers to its resemblance to pyromorphite. The colour varies from shades of green (pyromorphite) to yellow and brown (mimetite). Vanadinite is related to pyromorphite and mimetite, but much rarer, it is named for its content of the rare metal vanadium. No known magical correspondences.

**Scorodite:** Forms pyramidal, tabular or prismatic crystals of pale green, blue-green to blue and brown. Usually found as a secondary mineral formed by the alteration of arsenic minerals, especially arseno-pyrite. No known magical correspondences.

**Torbernite** and **Metatorbernite**: At atmospheric temperatures torbernite loses some of its water and tends to form metator-bernite. Found as secondary minerals in the oxidised zone of veins containing copper minerals and uraninite usually associated with other secondary uranium minerals. No known magical correspondences.

**Turquoise:** A distinctive sky-blue, bluish-green to apple-green gemstone, it is a secondary mineral formed by the action of surface waters, usually in arid regions on aluminous igneous and sedimentary rocks. Usually forming in veins or irregular patches in the rock. **TURQUOISE** is one of the earliest known gemstones mentioned in the lapidaries, and a sacred stone for many of the Native American people who believed it brought courage in battle. Brings protection against magical and psychic attack (especially for children), increases clairvoyance, telepathy and scrying, It also preserves from poisons and riding accidents. Small nodules of **HOWLITE** can also be found in gypsum deposits. This is white with marbly veining that is often dyed turquoise and used as a cheaper substitute for the real thing. Howlite does have its own magical uses in that it is a calming stone and helps to increase memory power and the ability to retain information — and increases the desire to amass knowledge.

## Turquoise Talisman

Although classed as a semi-precious gemstone, magically the humble turquoise can be much more protective than many other priceless stones. This should be given as a talisman to anyone who regularly comes into danger, particularly the armed forces and in equine pursuits. The talisman differs from an amulet (which is often a general good luck charm) because it has been magically endowed to protect from a specific danger. The talisman should be carried at all times until the specific danger is passed — ideally in a small leather pouch to be worn around the neck.

**Variscite** and **Strengite**: Rare crystals usually found as nodules and crusts. Variscite comes in various shades or green and strengite, violet or red, with white streaks, they are secondary phosphate minerals found in near-surface deposits. **VARISCITE** has crystallised water attached to its chemical structure and if exposed to sunlight, this water will evaporate — which means it can be assigned to Elemental Water.

**Vivianite:** The crystals are usually prismatic, sometimes flattened and blade-like, or encrusting masses with a fibrous structure. Colourless and transparent when fresh, becoming green, pale to dark blue by oxidisation. Found as a secondary mineral in the oxidised zone of metallic ore deposits containing iron sulphides, also in weathered zones of phosphate-rich and sedimentary rocks, especially those containing organic matter. **VIVIANITE** is a beautiful mineral that forms in rocks that contain the bones of animals. It needs special care because it will change colour on exposure to light or air and as such can be assigned to Elemental Air

**Wavellite:** Crystals are rare, usually occurring as hemispherical or globular. Occurs as a secondary mineral found on joint surfaces and in cavities of low-grade metamorphic rocks such as slates and in some sedimentary phosphate rock deposits. Sometimes found in limonitic-ore bodies. No known magical correspondences.

**Xenotime:** Forms short to long prismatic crystals, closely resembling ZIRCON with which it is often found in parallel growth. Its name in Greek means 'vain honour'. No known magical correspondences.

## Silicates

**The silicate minerals constitute almost a third of known minerals and form over 90% of the Earth's crust ... feldspar minerals and quartz being the most common ...** *(Pocket Guide to Minerals)*

**Allanite** (orthite): Commonly metamict, as a result of radiation damage caused by radioactive decay of thorium. Often weakly radioactive, the rock matrix around the crystals is often stained black as a result. No known magical correspondences.

**Andalusite:** The crystals are prismatic and nearly square, commonly pink or red and found in thermally metamorphosed rocks. Like ALEXANDRITE, **ANDALUSITE** changes colour in certain light and has an interesting variety called 'chiastolite', which, when sliced through, shows a clearly defined image of a cross. This shape changes pattern with each slice and because of this unusual property, the gem was once worn as an amulet to protect from evil spirits. Its first recorded usage was in Spain during the 16th century.

**Benitoite:** Rare crystals of blue, purple and white. Superb blue crystals are found in association with neptunite and natrolite on SERPENTINE. Fluoresces under short-wave ultra-violet light. Although **BENITOITE** may take on a wide range of colours, it has no true colour of its own; its colour dispersion is almost as striking as that of a diamond, which makes it ideal in scrying for purposes of revelation and inspiration.

**Beryl:** Named for its content of the rare metal beryllium, although it is for its value as a gemstone that it is better known. Gem varieties are **AQUAMARINE** (blue-green) used magically for concealment, courage and mental ability. The gem was carried by the Greeks and Romans in the form of amulets engraved with maritime themes as it was believed to afford protection on sea journeys. It was also considered a lucky stone for lovers, and was once prescribed by alchemists for healing toothache, epilepsy and diseases of the liver. **HELIODOR** (yellow) with its luminous golden rays represents purity, independence and initiative. The name heliodor comes from Greek meaning 'gift of the Sun'; **MORGANITE**, which is a pink variety of beryl was named after the American financier who bequeathed his famous gemstone and mineral collection to the New York Museum of Natural History, and not after the sister of King Arthur! An **EMERALD** with its characteristic deep green colour, when suspended from the neck was said to ward of malaria, sharpen the wits and quicken the intelligence, improved eyesight and to prevent epileptic seizures. **Medicinal:** It was also credited with curing moods of frenzy and those of lust and licence, as well as calming tempests in the sky. **Magical:** An emerald was also prescribed in cases of demonical possession, as an antidote to poison and poisoned wounds; it was believed to 'foreshow future events' and endowed the wearer with 'supernatural fore-knowledge'. "As a revealer of truth, this stone was an enemy of all enchantments and conjurations; hence it was greatly favoured by magicians, who found all their arts of no avail if an emerald were in their vicinity when they began to weave their spells"(Morales, "De las piedras preciosas", Valladolid, 1604). **BERYL** was believed to cure diseases of the eyes, spasms and convulsions; also reawaken love in married people. **Magical:** Worn to give help against "foes in battle and litigation; the wearer was rendered unconquerable and at the same time amiable, while his intellect was quickened and he was cured of laziness" ([*ibid*].

**Cordierite** (dichroite): Named after the French geologist, P. L. A. Cordier, who first found the mineral. Formed by medium to high-grade metamorphism of aluminium-rich rocks. A gem variety, **IOLITE** (from the Greek meaning 'violet stone) or **WATER SAPPHIRE** comes from gem gravels in Sir Lanka and Burma, or from Finland where it has been mined since prehistoric times. It was also a component of sacred sculptures and amulets of the Native American peoples long before the arrival of Columbus in 1492. This stone is sometimes called 'the stone of witchcraft' as it is reputed to enhance the occult powers of the wearer, by ensuring that any learning results in the increase of Wisdom. Iolite has the capacity to change colour depending on the angle from which it is viewed and the direction of the light source. This optical effect was used by Norse sailors to ascertain the position of the sun on overcast days, and is sometimes known as 'the Viking's compass'.

**Danburite:** Usually found in high-temperature deposits, either in veins or contact-metamorphosed rocks, growing free in pockets or embedded in rock and resembling TOPAZ. The most spectacular **DANBURITE** crystals are those from Miyazaki in Japan. This stone is said to resonate with the highest of spiritual energies and stimulates the Third Eye and Crown Chakra.

**Dioptase:** Short to long prismatic emerald green crystals. Occasionally found in oxidised zones of copper deposits, sometimes as well-developed crystals associated with other copper minerals and CALCITE. **DIOPTASE** is a fiery gemstone that is rare and very valuable; the green of the stone is sometimes so strong that it hides the magnificent sparkle. Use for scrying purposes and divination.

**Epidote group:** Includes zoisite, which comes in a variety of colours including pink (thulite) and purple (tanzanite); clinozoisite (pale green or greenish-grey) and epidote (yellowish-green to black). Prismatic crystals of epidote up to 20 cm long have been found. The variant forms are cut into gemstones. No known magical correspondences.

**Euclase** and **Gadolinite**: The former is usually found as rare prismatic crystals, associated with BERYL, and is one of the world's rarest and most valuable gemstones. The latter are massive prismatic crystals, black or sometimes brown, frequently associated with allanite. No known magical correspondences.

**Eudialyte:** Usually embedded in rock, with the grains occasionally showing a few free crystal faces, but always surrounded by other minerals. Brick-red, pink and brown this stone is a complex silicate of calcium, sodium, zirconium, cerium, iron and manganese. This is one of the rarer minerals but one that is attractive and popular with collectors. Magically, **EUDIALYTE** helps increase happiness, enjoyment of life, and the shaking free of a restricting lifestyle.

**Garnet group:** Found in metamorphic rocks, usually forming as isolated crystals. **PYROPE** (a magnesium garnet, named from the Greek *pyropos*, meaning 'fiery-eyed') is associated with Elemental Fire. The presence of pyrope garnet in certain rocks indicates that diamonds may be close by; **ALMANDINE** (an iron garnet) is usually darker than pyrope garnet, and many contain inclusions made of RUTILE or hornblende. When almandines that contain them are cut in cabochons they often display an *asterism* or four-pointed star (see STAR RUBY), which enhances their magical value. Spessartine (a manganese garnet) are usually shades of deep red and brown, to nearly black. Grossular (a calcium garnet — named from the Latin *grossular*, meaning 'gooseberry') is pale green, brown or white. **HESSONITE** is a brown, orange or yellow variety of grossular garnet and has been used for amulets and jewellery since ancient times. It is also known as essonite or cinnamon stone. Andradite (a calcium-iron garnet, named after the Portuguese minerologist J. B. de Andrade) can be yellow, brown or black. Uvaroviter (a calcium-chromium garnet, named after Count S. S. Uvarov, a Russian statesman and amateur mineral collector) is emerald green. Clear crystals are frequently cut as gemstones. One of the green **DEMANTOID** garnet's features is the way it reflects light — it seems to have many brightly-coloured lights trapped beneath the surface. Gem cutters make the most of this natural phenomenon by using special cutting techniques to highlight this 'flame' or 'fire' effect. Attuned to Elemental Fire. **GARNET**: A gemstone reputed to balance and activate the heart chakra, promote self-confidence and a love of life and magically attuned to the Element of Earth and the Element of Fire. The garnet possessed some wonderful virtues and guarded its wearer from all dangers, enabled them to vanquish all terrestrial obstacles and endows with a bold heart. Despite all the supposed advantages, however, Girolamo Cardano records (*De subtilitate*, 1560) that while wearing this stone he had many misfortunes that could not be traced to any error of his own.

## Stones of Blood

Red stones such as rubies, carbuncles (mythical, self-luminous fiery-red gems said to be the eyes of dragons) and garnets were believed to confer invulnerability from wounds. Some Asiatic tribes used garnets as bullets, 'upon the contrary principle that this blood-coloured stone would inflict a more deadly wound than would a leaden bullet'. Such bullets were used on the Kashmir frontier in 1892 by the Hanzas, and many of these precious missiles were preserved as curiosities by British troops *The Curious Lore of Precious Stones*, George Frederick Kunz.

**Hemimorphite** (calamine): A secondary mineral found in the oxidised zone of zinc-bearing ore, usually very close to the surface. Also associated with GALENA, SPHALERITE, smith-sonite, CERUSSITE and anglesite. The name calamine is also applied to smithsonite. No known magical correspondences.

**Humite series:** This group comprises four minerals: norbergite, chondrodite, humite and clinohumite and differ in the amounts of magnesia and silica they contain. Found typically in metamor-phosed dolomite limestones in association with SPINEL, phlogopite, GARNET, diopside and IDOCRASE. No known magical correspondences.

**Idocrase** (Vesuvianite]) Named from the Greek *eidos*, meaning 'form' and *krasis* meaning 'mixture' because the crystal forms appear to be a mixture of two minerals. **VESUVIANITE** is often found in blocks of dolomitic limestone erupted from Mount Vesuvius. It may be brown, dark green or yellow in colour and was first classified as a species in 1795 and can now be found in other locations.

**Ilvaite** and **Bertrandite:** In the former, the black crystals are prismatic and diamond-shaped; found chiefly as a contact metasomatic mineral in iron-zinc and copper ore deposits. The latter are small tabular or prismatic crystals, colourless to pale yellow, often as heart-shaped twins and associated with BERYL. **ILVAITE** is an unusual crystal that contains two different forms of the same metallic element and can be said to represent both sides of an argument or dispute.

**Kyanite:** Named from the Greek *kyanos*, meaning 'dark blue' for its customary colour; it usually occurs in long thin blade-like crystals, which are sometimes cut as gemstones. Typically found in medium to high-grade regionally metamorphosed schists and gneisses, **KYANITE** is associated with GARNET, STAUROLITE, mica and QUARTZ. This stone is said to realign the chakras and prepare the mind for meditation, or transmit healing energy. Helps overcome shyness and diffidence, encourages self-confidence.

**Olivine:** A rock-forming mineral, the name comes from the typical olive green colour of the crystals and the transparent gemstone **PERIDOT** (or chrysolite) has been mined for at least 3,500 years and was described by the Roman historian Pliny the Elder. The oldest recorded source was the rich deposit on the Egyptian island of Jazirat Zabarjed in the Red Sea. It was from there that the Crusaders first brought peridot to Europe in the 12th century. Used to draw wealth and reputed to help the wearer to banish demons and control other negative energies. Used to encourage mental clarity, aid visualisation, transformation. **CHRYSOLITE**, if 'worn on the bristle of an ass drives away demons and evil phantoms' and the finest were found in Egypt. To exert its full powers, the stone should be set in gold; worn this way will disperse 'the vague terrors of the night' and dissolve enchantments.

**Pectolite:** Chiefly found in basaltic rocks, often in association with zeolites; less commonly in calcium-rich metamorphic rocks and some alkaline igneous rocks. The most valuable **PECTOLITE** specimens display the attractive optical phenomenon known as 'cat's eye. It is sometimes known as **LARIMAR**.

**Phenakite:** A rare beryllium mineral found in cavities in granite in association with BERYL, TOPAZ and APATITE. The finest specimens are gem quality and because of their great brilliance, are sometimes mistaken for diamonds. The name **PHENAKITE** comes from the Greek *phenax*, meaning 'cheat' or 'deceiver' because the mineral may also be easily mistaken for quartz.

Could be used in charms for illusion or deceit.

**Piemontite** (piedmontite): A rare mineral found in some low-grade schists, and also in metasomatic manganese-ore deposits. It is reddish-brown to reddish-black, transparent to nearly opaque. Gem-quality stones are very rare and very valuable. No known magical correspondences.

**Sillimanite** (fibrolite): Commonly occurs as elongated prismatic crystals and is found in schist and gneisses produced by high-grade regional metamorphism. No known magical correspondences.

**Sphene** (titanite): The name originates from the Greek *sphen*, meaning 'a wedge' and referring to the actual shape of the crystals. Transparent specimens of **SPHENE** are sometimes cut as gemstones — faceted stones are fiery and brilliant. The most striking characteristic is its strong fire: it disperses the seen spectral colours that make up white light even more effectively than diamond. The optical properties of the stone are so striking that it would be one of the world's most precious gemstones if it were harder and more resilient to wear and tear.

**Staurolite:** Named from the Greek *stauros*, meaning 'cross' for its common and characteristic cross-like twinned form. It occurs frequently with GARNET, TOURMALINE, KYANITE or stillimanite in aluminium-rich metamorphic rocks. Some **STAUROLITE** is gem quality and the finest, twinned crystals that intersect at right angles may be fashioned for use as ornamental crosses.

**Topaz:** Its name deriving partly from a legendry island Topasos in the Red Sea, and partly from *tapas*, the Sanskrit word for 'fire'. The crystals are prized as gemstones, with the wine-yellow stones from Brazil being of particular value. Associated with FLOURITE, TOURMALINE, APATITE, BERYL and cassiterite and found as rounded pebbles or grains in alluvial deposits. **Medicinal: TOPAZ** was thought to be a healing stone for jaundice and to fortify the nerves. **Magical:** It brings strength and optimism, aids glamouring and fascination, and bestows charisma; the stone of nobility, honour and benevolence. **BLUE TOPAZ** is a light blue stone that holds the powers of Moon and Elemental Water with a soothing, calming effect; carry both solar and lunar crystals for a balance of energies.

## True or False

If topaz is naturally coloured, it has acquired that colour as a result of the crystal having been located in a part of the Earth adjacent to some radioactive element (e.g. autunite). A lot of colourless topaz is artificially irradiated and heat-treated to turn it blue — which renders it very difficult to distinguish from the more valuable gemstone aquamarine. Although natural radiation may take millions of years to have an effect on minerals, artificial irradiation techniques can change the colour of a gemstone in a matter of hours. In some case, the latter will later fade or revert completely to the original colour.
(*Treasures of the Earth*, Chris Pellant)

**Willemite:** Found as small prismatic or rhombohedral crystals in the oxidised zone of some zinc-ore deposits. It will often show strong fluorescence in ultra-violet light. No known magical correspondences.

**Wollastonite:** Formed by the metamorphism of siliceous limestones, both in contact aureoles or in high-grade regionally metamorphosed rocks usually associated with CALCITE, epidote, grossular and tremolite. No known magical correspondences.

**Zircon:** Named for its content of the rare metal zirconium, it is found as grains in gravels and sands. It is usually reddish brown with a vitreous lustre and good specimens are cut as the gemstone hyacinth. **ZIRCON** is often radioactive due to thorium and uranium replacing zirconium. Known from medieval times as **JACINTH**, the powdered stones were used in medicine as part of the infamous 'Most Noble Electuary of Jacinth'. **Medicinal:** The stone, worn either on the neck or the index finger would keep its owner free from plague and as an antidote to poison. It was also an amulet for travellers as a protection against the plague, wounds and injuries, and guaranteed the wearer a cordial reception at any hostelry. **Magical:** Used to help recognise that which is hidden and to promote health and wealth.

## Pyroxene Group
**A widely distributed group of rock-forming silicates, including the Orthopyroxenes: enstatite and hypersthene, found in basic and ultra-basic rocks poor in calcium, such as pyroxenites, peridotites and norites.**

**Aegirine:** Usually found as slender prismatic crystals, usually dark green of black; occurring in sodium-rich igneous rocks. No known magical correspondences.

**Clinopyroxenes: Dioside-Hedenbergite-Augite Series:**
Dioside crystals are usually stout prisms of square or octagonal cross-section. Replacement of magnesium by iron gives a series grading into hedenbergite.

Augite is similar to dioside and hedenbergite but contains aluminium and is a dark green to black constituent of many igneous rocks such as basalt, and peridotites. No known magical correspondences.

**Diopside:** A white-green mineral found in igneous rocks and metamorphosed impure dolomites. Diopside — the basic gemstone material of which **VIOLANE** is a variant — is made up of the elements calcium, magnesium, silicon and oxygen. Violene (from the Italian for 'violet') contains all of these elements, but the magnesium is substituted to some degree by manganese — the greater the concentration of manganese, the more intense the violet colouring will appear. No known magical correspondences apart from its healing potential.

**Enstatite:** Pale green in colour but darkening with increasing iron content to olive-green and brown. **ENSTATITE** is found in all the main types of rock and has also been found in meteorites. Its name comes from the Greek *enstates*, meaning 'adversary' — a reference to its high resistance to heat. Some transparent crystals of enstatite are coloured brown by the presence of iron; such specimens may also display a distinctive star-like optical effect known as *asterism*, which may be enhanced by careful cutting (see STAR SAPPHIRE). This variety is sometimes known as **BRONZITE.** Use magically to create an amulet to ward off psychic attack or any other unwelcome attention by 'fighting fire with fire'.

**Jadeite:** Various shades of light and dark green, sometimes white or lilac. Formed at high pressures and occurs in metamorphosed sediments and volcanic rocks. The name 'JADE' is used for the semi-precious stone is applied to two distinct minerals, jadeite and nephrite (an amphibole). **JADE** is a good luck stone and the personal luck is increased by the figure depicted in the carving; also promotes longevity. It is a stone to attract wealth and as such, should be handled every day. The green gem-quality form is known as Imperial Jade. **NEPHRITE** is less highly valued than jadeite, and is used in crystal therapy to aid the function of the kidneys (see Tremolite-Actinolite). Anyone possessing a small piece of jade should carry it with them at all times, as repeated handling absorbs 'something of its secret virtue into the body of the wearer. In China, pieces of jade were put into the foundations of a house to protect the family from lightening strikes. The Spanish *conquistadors* discovered jadeite deposits in Central America in the 16th century. They believed that it cured illnesses of the hip and kidney and called it *piedra de hijada* (loin stone) or *piedra de los rinones* (kidney stone).

**Spodemene**: Structurally related to the pyroxenes, this mineral is white or grey in colour and is translucent, but some varieties are transparent; fine lilac-coloured crystals known as **KUNZITE**, which is said to encourage joy and release negative energy. It is also said to help dispense pain whether physical or emotional. Give as an amulet to those suffering from severe mental problems. Deep-green crystals known as **HIDDENITE**, are cut as gemstones. Lithium salts, which are extracted from hiddenite and all other forms of spodumene, are widely used in psychiatric medicine to treat manic depression. The name **SPODUMENE** derives from the Greek *spodousthai,* meaning 'to be reduced to ashes' — referring to what happens when the mineral is heated under severe heat.

## Jade Charm

Jade can be used as an amulet to boost courage, bring good health and prevent misfortune. Jade is also used in spells to attract wealth, and should be added to any charm bag for this purpose; it is said that to increase wealth, the jade charm should be handled every day. The generic terms for all of the many Chinese 'wealth gods' is Ts'ai Shen, who should be petitioned for modest prosperity — a small jade figure of a tiger purchased on the last day of the old Chinese year would be considered a powerful charm when asking for monetary gain and health in daily routines.

(*Chinese Gods: The Unseen World of Spirits & Demons*, Keith Stevens)

## Amphibole Group
**Widely distributed in igneous and metamorphic rocks, it is similar to the pyrexenes group.** *(The Illustrated Encyclopaedia of Minerals)*

**Anthophyllite:** Typically found in medium-grade magnesium-rich metamorphic rocks, often associated with talc or cordierite. No known magical correspondences.

**Cummingtonite:** Found in calcium poor, iron-rich medium-grade metamorphic rocks, often in association with ore deposits. No known magical correspondences.

### Glaucophane-Riebeckite Series:
Gloucophane is typically found in sodium-rich schists formed by low temperature, high-pressure metamorphism; usually associated with JADEITE, ARAGONITE, CHLORITE, and GARNET. Riebeckite is a variety rich in iron that occurs mainly in alkaline igneous rocks. No known magical correspondences.

**Hornblende:** Usually prismatic and often with six-sided cross sections, it is a common rock-forming mineral found in both igneous and metamorphic rocks. No known magical correspondences.

**Rhodonite:** A distinctive pink to rose-red crystal, often veined by black. Commonly found with manganese-ore deposits. **RHONDONITE** is reputed to bring inspiration, helps recognise hidden talents and brings harmony.

**Tremolite-Actinolite:** The colour varies from white to green; darker green varieties occur due to the substitution of iron for magnesium, forming the variety known as actinolite. A very tough compact variety of tremolite or actinolite is the green coloured **JADE**, which is widely used as an ornamental stone. Jade also emits a vibrant, long-lasting note when struck, which would ensure the wearer's voice would become 'fully melodious'. Jade was prescribed for kidney troubles (including breaking up kidney stones) and all ailments of the urinary tract. Another kind of jade is the pyroxene jadeite (see **Jadeite**).

## Rhondonite Amulet

A deep red, transparent rhondonite crystal (often mistaken for rhodochrosite) from Australia would be the perfect charm for someone engaged in an arts project, or studying for exams. The stone helps to encourage inspiration and creativity in much the same way as zincite, but without the latter's debilitating effects, and helps develop hidden talents. Present the amulet in a red velvet pouch tied with silver cord or ribbon.

## Mica Group

**The micas belong to a group of minerals whose most obvious characteristic is the perfect cleavage by means of which the minerals may be split into leaves thinner than sheets of paper.** *(The Illustrated Encyclopaedia of Minerals)*

**Apophtyllite:** Occurs in association with zeolites in cavities in basalt, commonly associated with prehnite, analcime, stilbite and calcite. Found less commonly in cavities in some granite, gneiss and limestones. No known magical correspondences.

**Biotite:** Named after the French naturalist, J. B. Biott and one of the common rock-forming minerals and is found in almost all igneous rocks on a small scale. Phlogopite is found in metamorphosed limestones and magnesium-rich igneous rocks. No known magical correspondences.

**Chlorite group:** Crystals are generally green coloured, although violet and brown varieties are known. Often found in igneous rocks as an alteration product of pyroxenes, amphiboles and micas. Kaolinite is a secondary mineral produced by the alteration of aluminous silicates, especially the alkali feldspars. No known magical correspondences.

**Lepidolite:** Named for the Greek *lepidos*, meaning 'scale', it has a characteristic pale lilac colour, but is sometimes colourless, pale yellow or grey. Often found with lithium-bearing TOURMALINE, **LEPIDOLITE** is said to bring peace and harmony, reconciliation and a release from tension.

**Muscovite:** The name derives from the old name for Russia, Muscovy, for this colourless or pale coloured material. No known magical correspondences.

## Worry Stones

A worry stone, or worry beads, provides an object for the hands to play with in order to relieve mental tension. A worry stone in the form of a marble, jade or onyx egg/sphere should be small and smooth enough to be passed between the hands comfortably. Worry beads can be purchased complete or made especially from appropriate drilled stones reputed to bring peace and harmony. These relaxation techniques have been in use for hundreds of years in the East and Middle East, and can help relieve tension, arthritis and repetitive strain injury.

## Serpentine Group

The name applies to material containing one or more of the minerals chrysotile, antigorite (bowenite) and lizardite. Formed by the alteration of OLIVINE and enstatite under conditions of low to medium-grade metamorphism. **SERPENTINE** comes in many colours and under a variety of names — used in healing to calm mood swings and to disperse negative energy, i.e.

**LIZARDITE** was worn or carried against serpents and demonic possession, and to increase personal protection. The names of both are derived from their snake-like surface patterns.

**Talc** (steatite or soapstone): Found as a secondary mineral formed as a result of the alteration of olivine, pyroxene and amphibole, often lining faults in basic rocks. **STEATITE**, or soapstone as it is commonly known, is the massive variety of talc. It has been widely used throughout history to make carvings and ornaments — among the most famous surviving examples are cylindrical Assyrian seals, Chinese statues and Egyptian scarabs.

**Vermiculite:** A yellow or brown mineral with a pearly lustre; found as an alteration product of magnesium micas. Illite is a clay mineral present in shales and sediments: glauconite is formed usually in marine sedimentary rocks and sepiolite is a secondary mineral often associated with serpentine. No known magical correspondences.

## Serpentine

These stones are usually green with streaks or veins of white similar to a serpent's skin. It was believed that if anyone bitten by a snake, the stone should be applied to the wound to draw out the poison. For the cure to be effective, the stone must not be shaped or polished but remain in its natural state. It was also held that the touch of iron would destroy the magic efficacy of the substance of the stone.

## Silica Group

**The Silica group contains a number of minerals whose chemical composition is silicon dioxide. Quartz, tridymite and cristobalite are crystalline silica while chalcedony, jasper, flint and opal are cryptocrystalline silica (i.e formed of microscopic crystalline particles).** *(The Illustrated Encyclopaedia of Minerals)*

**Chalcedony: AGATE** is a variegated chalcedony with colour bands in concentric forms, usually following the outline of the cavity in which the mineral as formed. The colours are found in shades of white, grey, green, brown, red or black. It is worn to bring victory. Agate has a number of powers ascribed to it, among them being the ability to attract whatever woman one may desire and the faculty of shielding its owner from all danger. Additionally it made its wearer agreeable company to everyone, persuasive to all and favoured by God. Still further it cured insomnia, brought pleasant dreams, conferred a bold heart and overcame any and all obstacles, even acting as protection against the most evil of Evil Eyes: 'eye-agates', which had a white ring in the centre, were especially useful for that purpose. Agates were accredited with fire prevention and cooling properties, and attuned to Elemental Air. **Medicinal:** Agate is believed to be so powerful an absorbent that it can cure all manner of ills and conditions, with every type is 'prophylactic, bestowing on the wearer ability, grace, persuasive power, and a fine complexion'. **Magical:** A powerful protector against negative forces and the darker elements of magic; also 'averts tempests and influences the flow of rivers' **close gapMOSS AGATE** (or mocha stone) is chalcedony containing dark moss-like forms and is used to promote harmony and stability. Used to break enchantments, see through delusion and reveal duplicity. Translucent or transparent with masses of green moss-like filaments within that are completely inorganic in origin. **ENHYDROUS AGATE** is a rare crystal that contains liquid that was trapped when the rocks were formed — in magical terms, it combines the powers of Elemental Air and Elemental Water and an excellent aid to shamanic purposes. **BLACK AGATE** is used as an amulet against the powers of darkness, and to give courage and success. By contrast, **BLUE LACE AGATE** is the stone of peace and calmness, reduces tension, despite having its origins in volcanic lava such as basalt. **FIRE AGATE** displays a slightly different variation, displaying a rainbow-like play of surface colours caused by fragments of iron oxide. Found in rocks that originally formed through volcanic activity deep beneath the surface of the Earth it is magically attuned to Elemental Fire. **ONYX**, like agate, is banded chalcedony, but in this case the banding is straight and in parallel layers — brown and white banding being the most common. Much so-called onyx is, in fact, layered CALCITE. Onyx was thought to bring nightmares, fear and misfortune to its owner. If worn at the neck it was said to cool the ardour of love by provoking discord and separation of lovers. **BLACK ONYX** is used in the darker elements of magic guards against enemy attack and brings endurance and hope in the face of adversity. Believed to be generated in the clouds, onyx was said to protect against all diseases that arise from the air. **CHALCEDONY** is actually another form of quartz that comes in many colours. **Medical:** Dissipates the evil humours of the eye. **Magical:** Has the power to drive away 'phantoms and visions of the night'. **YELLOW CHALCEDONY** has been used to make ornaments and amulets for more than 2000 years; the finest artefacts are among the world's most art treasurers.

## Preparing an agate amulet

**Red** agate protects against spiders and scorpions

**Green** agate drives away eye diseases

**Tawny** or **brown** agate makes a warrior victorious; protects against poisonous reptiles; gives a lover favour in the sight of his lady; cures diseases; gives riches; increases intelligence; reduces menstruation; protects against the Evil Eye.

**Grey** agate worn around the neck prevents stiff neck and colic.

**Moss** agate should be worn on the upper arm to increase the vegetative powers of your plants and trees.

**Black** agate with veins is good for the heart.

To make an amulet you will need about ten inches of 18-guage silver wire to wrap around the stone just as you would wrap a parcel — from side to side and from top to bottom. When you are sure the stone cannot fall out, create a loop at the top by winding the wire around a thin pencil. Weave the wire back through the cage and when it is secure, remove the pencil, leaving the loop open enough to thread through a key ring, piece of cord or neck chain — or placed in a small pouch to be carried around in a handbag or briefcase.

(*How to Make Amulets, Charms & Talismans*, Deborah Lippman and Paul Colin)


**Chert:** A hard, yet brittle stone, usually a glassy dark grey, brown or black. The chert, FLINT and JASPER group all have microscopically grained QUARTZ, but these do not have the definite banding and the translucency of the CHALDEDONY group and usually have more impurities. **LYDDITE** (Lydian stone) is a dense black variety of chert, formerly used as a 'touchstone' used for determining the fineness (i.e purity) of gold and silver. Alchemically and magically used for detecting purity of intention or action. **FLINT** is hard and sharp and has often been used in weaponry; it represents the Fire of Earth since it was also used to create spark for fire lighting. Magically it is used to drive out negative energy, return ill-wishing to its sender and to cut through the bonds of enchantment (magical or emotional).


**Quartz:** The most common mineral in the Earth's crust, **QUARTZ** is the major constituent of the sand on a beach, and some rocks such as sandstone and quartzite. Usually colourless and transparent (**ROCK CRYSTAL**), or white and translucent (**MILKY QUARTZ**), coloured variations also occur and are frequently used as semi-precious stones. Magically used as shew stones or crystal balls, it also preserves its wearer from the terrors of the night. **ROSE QUARTZ** is a pale pink stone used to enliven the imagination, stimulate the intellect and enrich relationships. It has a very long history and known to have been used in making amulets since Roman times. It was believed to be a healing stone and the Romans used it in medicine. Some rose quartz crystals show a pronounced *asterism* when cut in cabochons (see STAR SAPPHIRE). **SMOKEY QUARTZ** is transparent and usually one of many shades of brown, and sometimes known by the name 'cairngorm' after the mountains in Scotland where some of the finest crystals are found. Black specimens are called **MORION QUARTZ** and both are used magically to clear the mind, banish confusion and allow access to the realms of Otherworld — a very special scrying stone. Although **IRIS QUARTZ** is basically colourless, the internal structure of the crystals enables it to diffract plain white light into the seven colours of the spectrum. Its properties was first described by the great Roman naturalist and historian Pliny the Elder (23-79 AD). Place under your pillow for untroubled sleep. **CARNELIAN** is an orange-red variety of quartz, its name deriving from the Latin *carneus*, meaning flesh-coloured. **Medical:** Gives the ability to speak boldly and well, as well as preserving the wearer from evil, the envious, and falling houses or walls. **Magical:** Used to boost all psychic and magical powers, restrains anger and gives courage in battle, and associated with Elemental Fire; **SARD** is brown quartz and has been used in jewellery since ancient Egyptian times — it is historically one of the most widely used of all gems. Regarded as a protection against incantations and sorcery, and believed to sharpen the wits of the wearer, rendering him fearless, victorious and happy. The red hue of this stone was supposed to neutralise the malign influence of the dark ONYX, driving away bad dreams, caused by the latter, and dispelling the melancholy thoughts it inspired. **CHRYSOPRASE** (or Prase) is a sparkling apple green 'victory stone' and prized for encouraging quick wits and adaptability; The deep violet **AMETHYST** was a well-known classic Greek preventive of drunkenness, and if water were poured into a vessel made of a amethyst-coloured stone, the liquid would appear like wine, and could be drunk with impunity. **Medical:** It insured that the owner would never be inflicted with blindness, nor troubled by strangulation or choking, gout and bad dreams; but it also offered protection against treason, and guarded one from deceit and imprisonment, **Magical:** It provided a shield against all enchantments, improved the complexion and prevented hair from falling out. This is the stone of the priesthood and used to increase spiritual power. The **BLOODSTONE** or **HELIOTROPE** is green with spots of red jasper and was considered ideal for stopping nosebleeds. **Medical:** It was also believed to preserve the faculties and bodily health of the wearer; make water boil, to produce rain, maintain a good reputation, expel poison, preserve health and vigour throughout life, to help foretell the future and to prevent one from being cheated. **Magical:** Most importantly, it could make the wearer invisible if used in conjunction with the plant called heliotrope, while reciting the proper incantation and performing the correct ritual. Increases spiritual awareness, confidence and intellectual creativity. The *Leyden Papyrus* says: "If anyone has this with him he will be given whatever he asks for; it also assuages the wrath of kings and despots, and whatever the wearer says he will be believed. Whoever bears this stone, which is a gem, and pronounces the name engraved upon it, will find all doors open, while bonds and stone walls will be rent asunder." **JASPER** is impure quartz, usually coloured red by hematite [**RED JASPER**] and was judged to assist childbirth if worn on the thigh, and was also thought to prevent haemorrhage during the birth process. **Medicinal:** Expectant mothers were advised to keep the stone on their person at all times as a defence against evil spirits and for maintaining purity of heart. Also encourages deep states of meditation and harmony, and known as the 'stone of good will' and unselfishness. Used in healing to reduce stress. Worn as an amulet against snakebites and headaches, lethargy and epilepsy. An amulet of **GREEN JASPER** is worn to protect against fevers and dropsy. **Magical:** The colour is at least important as chemical composition in determining the talismanic or therapeutic worth of the different stones; the great variety of colours and markings in the different jaspers indicate their use in many different ways. **SARDONYX** is a banded form of SARD, being a stone generated in the earth by the power and heat of the sun, was said to strengthen the intellect of its owner and to grant a superior degree of understanding and all senses of the body, and drives away anger, stupidity, and undisciplined passion. When worn consistently it eliminated stupidity, and calmed obstinate and unruly passions. **CITRINE** is a variety of quartz and derives its yellow colouration from the presence of minute inclusions of iron, hence its magical quality for dispersing (or 'earthing') negative energy and averting curses and bad luck; while **AMETRINE** is a combination of amethyst and citrine, used to reduce fear of change and to encourage inspiration. **TIGER'S EYE** is a rare form of black quartz that has yellow and golden brown stripes and is used to cast light on hidden subjects; it helps with astral visions and lucid dreaming.

## Amethyst Amulet

The amethyst is the sacred stone of the priesthood and symbolises the sephirah of Hod in the mystical Qabalah. According to *Liber 777*, it is the "purity of the Exempt Adept which destroys the illusion or drunkenness of existence, enabling him to take the great leap into the Abyss" — hence the claims for the stone protecting from drunkenness on a mundane level. It is believed to give "fortitude to those who are given responsibility for the spiritual leadership of others, hence the symbolic rings of bishops and popes are set with amethyst" (*The Gemstones Handbook*) — the ring of a pope being ritually destroyed on his death. Carry a 'hound's tooth' crystal in a pouch to increase spiritual and magical power. Also use in the 'rites of psychic cleansing, purification, consecration and preparation for initiatory experiences'.

**Opal:** This may be white, grey, yellow, red or brown, the colour often changing according to the direction in which the **OPAL** is viewed, displaying internal reflections known as 'opalescence'. The prized gem varieties are the Australian famous iridescent **BLUE OPAL**, and the Mexican bright orange-red colour, known as a **FIRE OPAL**. Hyalite is a clear glassy opal and wood opal is silicified wood in which silica has replaced branches of trees, preserving their external appearance and cellular structure. **Medical:** In medicine, the opal was thought of in the nature of a panacea because it possessed all the colours of all the stones, and was believed to have all of their curative powers as well. **Magical:** It is the 'stone of truth' and can reveal hidden knowledge. Used for spiritual journeys and inducing altered states of consciousness; it is attuned to Elemental Water. **WOOD OPAL** forms from trees that lived between 200 million and 20 million years ago. When the weight of the earth presses down on fallen trees and compresses them, the carbon they contained when alive has been replaced by opal-bearing fluids.

## Feldspar Group

**The feldspars are the most abundant of all minerals, accounting for nearly half the volume of the Earth's crust. Some FELDSPAR gives out subtle flashes of an almost metallic sheen and often considered to combine the dual energies of both male and female, i.e. androgynous.** *(The Illustrated Encyclopaedia of Minerals)*

**Axinite:** Crystals are usually tabular and wedge-shaped in a distinctive clove-brown colour, but sometimes yellow, pink or grey. Commonly found in calcareous rocks that have undergone contact metamorphism; also occurs in cavities in granites. **AXINITE** gets its name from the shape of its crystals, which often resemble tiny axes or hatchets. It is a beautiful but rare stone and magically would make an ideal focus for meditation over personal matters when a forceful approach is needed.

**Chrysocolla:** Various shades of blue, blue-green to green; sometimes brown or black when impure; a fairly common mineral in the oxidisation zone of some copper deposits. CHRYSOCOLLA takes several forms depending on the other minerals that are mixed with it. Legend has it that the eilat stone variety of this gemstone was originally found in King Solomon's Mines. Magically it is beneficial for relationships and cleanses the atmosphere after arguments. Associated with Elemental Earth it gives inner strength and courage.

**Dumortierite:** Rare as prismatic crystals and not a common mineral, this occurs in considerable amounts at a few locations containing aluminium-rich metamorphic rocks. Violet, pink-violet, or blue-purple stones are found in America in quartz concentrations in metamorphic rocks, and in gneisses and schists. The blue stone is often carved as imitation LAPIS LAZULI. DUMORTIERITE is used to deflect psychic attack and high-level energy fields. Can also encourage prophesy, lateral thinking, innovation and all metaphysical powers.

**Feldsparthoid** minerals are a group of sodium and potassium aluminosilicates, which are formed in place of feldspars when an alkali-rich magma is deficient in silica. No known magical correspondences.

**Hauyne** and **Nosean**: Found in silica-poor lavas such as phonolites and related igneous rocks in association with leucite or nepheline. No known magical correspondences.

**Lazurite:** A rare azure-blue mineral, usually occurring in crystalline limestones as a produce of contact metamorphism. Gem-quality crystals of **LAZULITE** are rare and highly prized by collectors; and its name like its colour, is closely related to lapis lazuli and derives from the Medieval Latin *lazulum*, meaning 'azure'. Although lapis lazuli is a composite gemstone, all genuine samples of it must contain the mineral lazurite. **LAPIS LAZULI** has provided the most expensive of medieval pigments — ultramarine being a powdered pigment from ground lapis lazuli, which has been used by painters since the Middle Ages — as well as an intrinsic element of ancient Babylonian and Egyptian jewellery and amulets. **Medical:** The 'blue stone with little gold spots' was a cure for melancholy and for the 'quartern fever'. **Magical:** Used to increase magical energy levels and strengthen psychic barriers against negative energies.

**Leucite:** Found embedded in potassium-rich silica-poor lavas, this white or grey mineral does not occur in plutonic igneous rocks. No known magical correspondences.

**Microcline** and **Orthoclase:** The former gets its name from the Greek *micro*, meaning 'small' and *kleinen*, meaning 'incline'; the latter comes from the Greek *orthos*, meaning 'right angle' and *klasis*, meaning 'fracture'. Amazonite is a green to bluish-green variety of microline. The green colour is produced by trace amounts of lead impurities in the normally white or pink microline; adularia is a glassy variety of orthoclase and moonstone has a bluish appearance. Sanidine occurs as small crystals in volcanic rocks. **MOONSTONE** or **SELENITE** brings good fortune — particularly to lovers — and is a sacred stone of India. **Medical:** It drives away sleep, but has magical properties that enable the owner to foretell the future although its powers waxed and waned with the moon. It could also help with business success and relieve any situation where a lack of confidence prevents success. **Magical:** An amulet brings strength and reconciliation between lovers. Moonstone has been known since the earliest times but it is not a strictly defined gem species, and almost any mineral can be described as moonstone as long as it has the basic optical properties: a blue colour and /or a distinctive play of light about its surface. Some historians have suggested that what early civilisations called moonstone was probably selenite, the transparent form of gypsum. Known to the ancient Egyptians as *neshmet*, **AMAZONITE** was one of the more important, but also rarer, gemstones used for jewellery. It was used for beads in pre-Dynastic times in Egypt, and especially popular for jewellery during the 12$^{th}$ and 18$^{th}$ Dynasties; during the Graeco-Roman periods it was also used for amulets. In modern psychic working it is used in meditation, to increase confidence and decrease stress. Also said to aid clairvoyance, mystic and spirit communications.

**Natroline:** Delicate prismatic crystals, commonly elongated and needle-like in compact masses, this occurs lining cavities in basaltic rocks. **NATROLITE** is one of the most spectacular zeolite minerals with its delicate radiating needle-shaped crystals it could be said to represent Elemental Air.

**Nepheline:** Six-sided prisms, commonly found as shapeless or irregular grains; they are characteristic minerals of silica-poor alkali igneous rocks of both plutonic and volcanic associations. A variety, **PHONOLITE** gives a metallic ring when struck and can give the wearer a melodious voice if worn around the neck. It also induced sweet sleep, free of bad dreams.

**Petalite:** Found in association with cleavelandite, QUARTZ and LEPIDOLITE, this colourless, white or grey mineral is found in 'large cleavable blocky masses'. No known magical correspondences.

**Plagioclase Feldspars** form a series from albite, through oligoclase, andesine, LABRADORITE, bytownite to anorthite and occur in many igneous rocks. **AVENTURINE** is a variety of oligoclase containing HEMATITE, which gives it the golden shimmer. Brings magical inspiration and the confidence to use psychic powers wisely. This can be a very personal crystal that can increase magical awareness. The stone has been used since the 3$^{rd}$ century AD for carving into a wide range of ornamental objects. **GREEN ADVENTURINE** — which may be sold under the name of Indian jade — is sometimes used to imitate the even more valuable JADEITE. It is composed mainly of QUARTZ and contains the magical qualities of that stone. **LABRADORITE** is said to bring the user a wealth of wisdom and understanding. It is sometimes viewed as a 'Temple of the Stars' so using it for scrying purposes can produce inner illumination and insight. This stone epitomises magical ability, helps to release the powers of the imagination, inhibition and false modesty. Reddish-golden inclusions in Norwegian and Canadian oligoclase reflect brilliantly to produce **SUNSTONE**. Used magically to promote vitality, increase energy; increases courage and ambition.

**Scapolite:** Found in metamorphosed limestone, these uneven prismatic crystals occur in skarns close to igneous contacts. Most scapolite is too soft to be used as jewellery and is only faceted for collectors. It is the gem variety of the mineral wernerite. No known magical correspondences.

**Sodalite:** Commonly azure-blue, also pink, yellow, green or grey-white. Often found associated with nepheline in alkali igneous rocks such as nepheline-syenites; also in some silica-poor dyke rocks and lavas. Some specimens show a reddish fluorescence in ultra-violet light. **SODALITE** gives courage and protection, lessens fear and increases strength — associated with the power of Elemental Water.

**Tourmaline:** The name comes from the Singhalese word *turamali* for gem pebbles. This is usually black in colour (schorl) if it comes from Devon and Cornwall, but also occurs as white, colourless (achroite), brown (dravite), pink (elbaite), and blue, frequently with colour zoning. Transparent gemstones have been cut as gemstones for many centuries, probably because the **TOURMALINE** shows a greater range of colour than any other gemstone. It was said to help bodily healing and to repair bone or sinew damage. Magically this helps to draw wealth and power; also aids regeneration and renewal. **GREEN TOURMALINE** reflects light in a way that is thought to be unique in the natural world and is attuned to Elemental Air. **INDICOLITE** is one of the rarest and most valuable members of the tourmaline family; usually azure or deep blue, although it may have discernible green tones. It has a brilliant sparkle and the Romans used it — particularly in amulets carved with the images of animals — and believed it to have strange occult powers. **RUBELLITE** is the name given to the pink or red transparent varieties of tourmaline. Like all forms of tourmaline when rubellite is subjected to mechanical stress an electrical charge passes through it and one end of the mineral takes on a positive charge, while the other end takes on a negative charge. Ideal for psychic balancing. **VERDELITE** derives its name from the French word *vert*, meaning 'green'. Some pieces show different colours depending on the direction of the light source and the angle from which they are viewed. An excellent stone for scrying.

## 'Sapphire of the Ancients'

Because of its variable components, lapis lazuli is not really a mineral at all, but a rock, although this does not prevent it from being one of the most highly prized of all gemstones known as the 'sapphires of the ancients'. In Egypt lapis lazuli was a favourite stone for amulets and ornaments such as scarabs; it was also used in Mesopotamia by the Sumerians, Akkadians, Assyrians, and Babylonians for seals and jewellery. Lapis jewellery has been found at excavations of the pre-dynastic Egyptian site Naqada (3300–3100 BC), and powdered lapis was used as eyeshadow by Cleopatra· In Mesopotamia, lapis artefacts can be found in great abundance, with many notable examples having been excavated at the Royal Cemetery of Ur (2600-2500 BC). Lapis has been collected from mines in the Badakhshan province of Afghanistan since the Stone Age and in antiquity, lapis lazuli was known as 'sapphire', which is the name used today for the blue corundum variety of gemstone. In ritual magic, the gold specks in it are said to be particles of dust from the cosmos and the stone itself symbolises the highest form of Jupiter.

## Zeolite Group

**Contains true water of crystallisation; one of the few minerals displaying reversible dehydration.** *(The Illustrated Encyclopaedia of Minerals)*

**Analcime:** White or grey, often tinged with pink, yellow or green, this is commonly found as a secondary mineral in cavities in basaltic rocks associated with other zeolites. **ANALCIME** crystals are highly prized by collectors and although they are of little practical use, they are among the most beautiful minerals on Earth. When heated they give off water. Attuned to Elemental Water.

**Chabazite:** Typically occurs lining cavities in basalts and andesites, associated with other zeolites. Usually white or yellow cube crystals, often pinkish or red. No known magical correspondences.

**Datolite:** Usually in short prismatic crystals, which often show a variety of forms. Colourless or pale shades of yellow and green, this is a secondary material, usually found in cavities in basic igneous rocks associated with zeolites, prehnites and CALCITE. Also in some veins and granites. **DATOLITE** is basically colourless but may be coloured by impurities. Its name is derived from the Greek *dateisthai*, meaning 'to divide' and as such could be used in a charm requiring division

**Heulandite:** Crystals are usually tabular or 'coffin shaped'. A common zeolite mineral, it is often associated with stilbite in cavities in basaltic rocks, and sometimes found in sedimentary rocks as a secondary mineral. No known magical correspondences.

**Laumonite:** Occurs with other zeolites in veins in igneous rocks. It is also produced as a result of very low-grade metamorphism of some sedimentary rocks and tufts. A characteristic alteration, laumonite loses part of its water on exposure to dry air and becomes powdery, friable and chalky (leonhardite). No known magical correspondences.

**Prehnite:** Occurs chiefly in cavities in basic igneous rocks often associated with zeolites; also in low-grade metamorphic rocks and as an alteration product in some altered igneous rocks. **PREHNITE** is often called 'the stone for dreaming and remembering', which can aid the awakening and strengthening of various clairvoyant abilities such as prophesy, scyring, etc.

**Stilbite:** Commonly found as sheaf-like aggregates in white, yellow or pink; sometimes brick red. Found in cavities in basalts, and associated with heulandite. No known magical correspondences.

**Thomsonite:** Associated with zeolites in cavities in basalts and related igneous rocks. Also found as an alteration product of nepheline, this often appears as a series of coloured rosettes. No known magical correspondences.

## Scrying with small stones

Even the smallest of gemstones in crystal form can be used for scrying providing there is a surface to attract a pinpoint of light (see Chapter Nine). The most effective are aquamarine, iolite, jade, leopard skin jasper, prehnite, jet, moonstone, quartz, smoky quartz and turquoise. Stones are also known to attract and hold psychic energies, so never allow those used for scrying to be handled by anyone else — keep in a pouch and out of sight.

It should be obvious from this extensive list of minerals that there is far more to the study of crystals than merely buying the expensive varieties sold in shops or by mail order for magical working. Not only do we have the geological associations to take into account, we also have a gem-lore dating back to those early lapidaries, which recorded the magical use of gemstones in the form of amulets and other magical/medicinal preparations.

More importantly, the list also shows that through 'metamorphism' and 'alteration' each mineral can develop different properties when in contact with other material. It also suggests that a variety of different 'magical correspondences' can be applied to each 'crystal' when it is used in association with its correct geological applications.

NB: This list of minerals and stones is not intended to substitute for a complete, analytical treatment of the subject. It is merely intended to provide a few of the highly visible characteristics (or magical correspondences) of the various minerals and the locations in which they may be found. Detailed and diagnostic descriptions may be found in many of the good field guides or from publishers who specialise in scientific works. If a more scientific interest develops in mineralogy and the collecting of the different minerals and

**gemstones, the best methods of keeping them is in specially made specimen boxes.**

## Try this exercise

A crystal pendulum used for dowsing, draws on an ancient knowledge for unlocking psychic power and seeking out information not easily available by any other means.

- Obtain a rock, quartz or plain glass crystal, cut and polished and fitted with a peg and ring. A neck chain means it can be discretely worn as a pendant. Simply slip it off and use the chain as a pendulum cord anywhere, anytime.

- Pendulums are still widely used to locate natural resources such as water and minerals. This can be done by walking around the area to see where the pendulum's strongest reaction occurs, or holding the pendulum over a map while concentrating on what is to be located. When contact is made the pendulum will begin to swing.

- Correct direction of the swinging pendulum will differ from one person to another: some users read the pendulum swinging in circles to the right means affirmative, and to the left negative. Some read affirmative for movements north-south as affirmative, and east-west negative. Others will interpret swinging from side to side as affirmative, and in a circle for negative.

- Once you have obtained a pendulum, begin to experiment with it. Hold your arm away from the body, and if necessary, prop it with the other arm to prevent it from shaking, as body tremors will distort the reading. Loop the chain or cord over the middle finger of the right hand and ask the pendulum for answers and direct how it should respond. The stronger the response, the more emphatic the answer.

It takes practice and patience to use a pendulum but once the signals for 'yes' and 'no' have been firmly established, this can be an extremely reliable form of divination — and one of the oldest means of psychic working. When not in use, keep the pendulum concealed in a pouch and away from curious fingers. *The Power of the Pendulum* by T. C. Lethbridge, provides in-depth information on the subject to aid further study.

## Chapter Five

# Apocalptica

The Middle Ages were truly the time of the lapidary, for we see his handiwork everywhere from royal regalia to the ornamentation of church furnishings. And it was during this time that the magical history of stones reached its most brilliant as the Western church adopted more and more of the blazing splendour of the Byzantine church in the East.

Other kinds of 'power objects' began to gain in popularity, such as the reliquaries containing the physical remains of sacred persons, or artefacts connected with sacred events. And almost anything imaginable might be found in them, from a piece of the true cross and the 'milk of Mary' to the blood and fingernails of a martyr. One of the most interesting being the Iron Crown of Lombardy (*Corona Ferrea*), which is both a reliquary and one of the most ancient royal insignia of Europe. The crown, now kept in the Cathedral of Monza in Milan, became one of the symbols of the Kingdom of Lombards and later of the medieval Kingdom of Italy. The Iron Crown gets its name from a narrow band of iron about one centimetre (three-eighths of an inch) said to be beaten out of one of the nails used at the crucifixion. The outer circlet of the crown is of six segments of beaten gold partly enamelled, joined together by hinges and set with 22 gemstones that stand out in relief, in the form of crosses and flowers. Its small size and hinged construction suggest that it was originally a large armlet or perhaps a votive crown; or a readjustment after the loss of two segments, as described in historical documents.

Nevertheless, wonder-working properties were ascribed to most of these relics, and many of them became the goals of pilgrimage.

Not in an altogether disinterested fashion the various shrines housed their artefacts and anatomical remnants in the most elaborate casings they could afford, and the goldsmiths and lapidaries rejoiced. Others were kept in elaborate purse-shaped receptacles of jewel-studded gold, in place of the customary cloth or leather, or in containers that reproduced an anatomical form when they held a fragment of a martyr's or saint's body. (*Riches of the Earth*, Frank J. Anderson)

The early Christian church held it to be acceptable to 'adore' a relic as a means of communion with the saint on whom it fixes the mind, and as a channel of divine power and grace — in an act of what would otherwise be termed as 'sympathetic magic'. By the $4^{th}$ century, the cult of relics was far advanced, and from the $9^{th}$ century, relics of the True Cross were housed in magnificent gold and silver cross-shaped reliquaries, decorated with enamels and some of the world's most fabulous gems. In the high Middle Ages, reliquaries grew ever more splendid as the faithful visited them, kissed them, be cured by them, and take oaths on them.

During the later Middle Ages, the *monstrance* was introduced — a form of reliquary that housed the relic in a rock crystal or glass capsule mounted on a rod, enabling the relic to be displayed to the faithful. Reliquaries in the form of personal jewellery also appeared around this time, housing tiny relics — such as pieces of the Holy Thorn; and it was only a step away to re-adopting the wearing of stones and crystals as magical amulets and talismans.

Surprisingly enough, this magical jewellery drew on the ancient world for its associations, and the virtues believed to be inherent in the precious stones were thought to have added potency when engraved with some sigil or image of something deemed to be sacred. One of the earliest images that still holds its potency today in esoteric circles is the Egyptian scarab that represents immortality and resurrection — with ancient amulets being carved out of jasper, amethyst, lapis-lazuli, ruby and carnelian.

Many of the engraved stones from Imperial Roman times were of the Egyptian gods Serapis and Isis, as the representations of Time and the Earth. On other stones were carved the symbols of the zodiac showing the natal constellation of the wearer and carried as amulets. These designs were usually engraved on onyx, carnelians or similar stones during Graeco-Roman times — but occasionally an emerald was used, and more rarely a ruby or sapphire. Nowhere in the ancient world was the use of amulets so common as in Alexandria, and the types produced there were scattered throughout the Roman world. Since the custom was deep-rooted in Egyptian culture, when Alexandria became a great commercial centre, it is not surprising that the population adopted "various amulets used by the adherents of the different religions" (*The BM Dictionary of Ancient Egypt*). The result was a combining and confusion of many different types produced on a commercial scale.

With the rapid rise of Christianity, this older element was retained, and despite leading Christian teachers being strongly opposed to such superstitious and pagan practices, the common people clung to old customs. The spreading of the Gnostic 'heresy' added a further dimension to the creation of amulets. With its interweaving of pagan and Christian doctrine, not to mention the complicated and often incomprehensible symbolism, the magical virtues of the sigils were enhanced by the purposely obscure inscriptions, which also spread throughout the Roman Empire. As an example, George Kunz cites the amulet in the Cabinet de Medailles in Paris, that shows the head of Alexander the Great, backed by a she-ass with a foal, and below this a scorpion and the name Jesus.

After the 4th century, what we now refer to as 'magical corre-spondences' began to impose themselves upon the preparation of amulets and talismans. The *images* engraved on the stones were held to have a greater or lesser degree of effectiveness, independent of the properties contained with the gemstones themselves. This effectiveness was also dependent upon the hour, day or month when the work was carried out; the influence of the planet, star or constellation which was in the ascendant at the time was also believe to infuse a subtle essence into the stone as the sigil or image was being engraved. To generate the maximum magical power, the virtue of the image *must* be of the same association as the virtue inherent in the stone — the amulet being less powerful when this was not the case.

For example, images symbolising zodiacal signs were deemed to have the powers invested in those signs, and the stones selected for engraving only enhanced the power if they were in sympathy with that particular sign. By medieval times, the idea of the magical qualities of all engraved gemstones had become so deeply rooted that in many cases a magical power was assigned to them that was entirely at odds with the original intention of the engraver.

*The Book of Wings*, compiled c13th century by Ragiel gives an account of the most popular designs with their appropriate stones. For example:

- The figure of a **dragon** engraved on a **ruby** or other stone of a similar nature has the power to "augment the goods of this world and make the wearer joyous and healthy."
- The image of **Poseidon in a chariot** engraved on a **beryl** will "preserve sailors unharmed by tumults."
- A **falcon** engraved on a **topaz** "helps to acquire the goodwill of kings, princes and magnates", i.e. influential people.
- An **astrolabe** (an astrological instrument) if engraved on a **sapphire** has the power to increase wealth and enable the wearer to predict the future.
- An image of a **lion** engraved on a **garnet** will protect and

preserve honour and health, cure the wearer of all disease, bring honour and protect the wearer from all perils while travelling.

- An **ass** engraved on a **chrysolite** will give the power to prognosticate and predict the future.
- The image of a **ram** (or **bearded man**) on a **sapphire** has "the power to cure and preserve from many infirmaties" (*The Curious Lore of Precious Stones*) as well as to free from poison and from all demons. This is a royal image; "it confers dignities and honours and exalts the wearer."
- A **frog** engraved on a **beryl** will have the power to reconcile enemies and produce friendship where there was discord.
- The image of a **camel's head**, or **two goats among myrtles**, if engraved on **onyx** has the power to "convoke [evoke], assemble and constrain demons; if anyone wears it, he will see terrible visions in sleep."
- A **vulture** engraved on a **chrysolite** has the power to constrain demons and the winds.
- A **bat** represented on a **heliotrope** or **bloodstone** gives the wearer power over demons and helps incantations.
- A **griffin** engraved on ro**ck crystal** produces an abundance of milk.
- A **man richly dressed and with a beautiful object in his hand** engraved on **carnelian**, checks the flow of blood and confers honours.
- A **lion** or an **archer** on **jasper** gives help against poison and cures from fever.
- A **man in armour, with bow and arrow**, engraved on an **iris** [*sic*] stone protects from evil both the wearer and the place where it may be. (Possibly meaning Isis = emerald).
- A **man with a sword in his hand** engraved on a **carnelian** preserves the "place where it may be from lightning

and tempest, and guards the wearer from vices and enchantments."

- A **bull** engraved on **prase** (chrysoprase) is said to give aid against evil spells and to procure the favour of magistrates.
- A **hopoo with a tarragon herb** before it, engraved on a **beryl** confers the power to invoke water-spirits and to converse with them as well as call up the mighty dead.
- A **horse** engraved on a **turquoise** will keep both mount and rider safe from mishap.
- A **swallow** engraved on a **celonite** establishes and preserves peace and concord among men.
- A **man with his right hand raised aloft**, if engraved on **chalcedony**, gives "success in lawsuits, renders the wearer healthy, gives him safety in his travels and preserves him from all evil chances.".
- The **names of God**, on a *curaunia* (?) stone, have the power to preserve the place where the stone may be from tempests; they also give the wearer victory over his enemies.
- A **bear** engraved on an **amethyst** has the virtue of putting demons to flight and defends and preserves the wearer from drunkenness.
- A **man in armour** engraved on a **magnet** (magnetite) or **lodestone**, has the power to aid in incantations and makes the wearer victorious in war.
- The image of a **tree** engraved on an **agate** will bring a good harvest if tied to the arm of the ploughman, or the horn of his ox.
- The image of a **scorpion** engraved on a **bezoar** stone when the moon is in Scorpio will protect against poison, especially in wounds.

The attributes of each stone in the listing shows that 13th century problems were mainly confined to protecting oneself from demons (what we would today call 'negative energy'), mishaps while travelling, and tempests. On the positive side, it was obvious that folk were still concerned about attracting wealth, but apart from the good offices of influential people, there is no mention of 'love charms' which pre-occupy modern books on crystal magic.

From a contemporary magical point of view, we can combine any of the above talismanic images together with the appropriate gemstone, using genuine 13<sup>th</sup> century antecedents. For example: the image of a horse engraved on a small piece of baking foil with a blunt pencil, and wrapped around a tiny piece of turquoise, is aimed at keeping both mount and rider safe from mishap if poked into a secure place in the underside of the rider's saddle.

## The Cult of Birthstones

The fashion for using 'birthstones' as personal amulets appears to have its origins in the twelve gemstones from the breastplate of the High-Priest and "the gems contributed for the tabernacle by the Israelists in the wilderness" (*The Curious Lore of Precious Stones*). There are two lists of twelve stones to be found in both the Old and New Testament but these do not correspond to the months of the year, or the zodiac, but to the twelve tribes of Israel, or the twelve mighty angels who guard the gates of Paradise. The following extract is given in Exodus (xxviii, 15-30) and quoted in *The Curious Lore of Precious Stones* — written by that distinguished mineralogist George Frederick Kunz (1856-1932) who, for more than 50 years was the gem expert for Tiffany's in New York:

> ... *And thou shalt set in its* [the breastplate] *settings of stones, even four rows of stones: the first row shall be sardius* [carnelian], *a topaz, and a carbuncle; this shall be the first row.*
>
> *And the second row shall be an emerald, a sapphire* [lapis lazuli?] *and a diamond* [rock crystal or corundum?]

*And the third row a ligure* [amber or jacinth], *an agate, and an amethyst.*

*And the fourth row a beryl, and an onyx, and a jasper; they shall be set in gold in their enclosings.*

Islamic legend also represents the various heavens as composed of different precious stones, and in the Middle Ages, these religious ideas became interwoven with a host of astrological, alchemical, magical and medical superstitions. There is, however, a much earlier Egyptian representation suggested by the breast-ornament worn by a High-Priest of Memphis, carved in a 14$^{th}$ Dynasty relief, consisting of 12 small balls or crosses. "As it cannot be determined that these figures were cut from precious stones, the only definite connection with the Hebrew ornament is the number of the figures; this suggests but fails to prove, a common origin," concluded George Frederick Kunz.

Many of the 'classical' lists cited as the antecedents for natal or zodiacal stones will include diamonds — but this gem could *not* have been one of the original stones because astrology dates back thousands of years and no one knew how to cut a diamond way back then. The art of cutting diamonds was only discovered a few hundred years ago, mainly because it takes a diamond to cut a diamond and the ancient lapidaries did not know this, and so the diamond could not have been among the zodiacal stones at that time. It may be possible that what was later mistaken for a diamond was more likely to have been rock crystal but this 'humble' stone may not have been considered valuable enough in later times. The ancient priesthood, however, would have known about the magical powers contained within the rock crystal, even if latter day folk did not.

Or as Kunz observed, "A mysterious stone mentioned three times in the Old Testament, each signifies a material noted for its hardness and translated 'diamond', however, as it is almost certain that the Hebrews were not familiar with the 'diamond' it was most probably a variety of corundum ..." Similarly, lapis lazuli was referred to as the 'sapphire of the ancients' and it may have been lapis rather than the rarer blue corundum (sapphire) variety that was in use at this time.

Birthstones are still used today as amulets to attract health, wealth and happiness and most people know their own birthstone but from the dozens of different compilations, which is the correct attribution for each month?

The origins of the cult of the birthstone and the belief that each stone was endowed with its own peculiar virtue for those born in that month can be traced back to the writings of Josephus (1st century AD) and St Jerome (5th century). Despite these early references, the common usage of giving and wearing a birthstone seems to have originated much later in Poland sometime during the 18th century. As Kunz tells us, the belief in the special virtues of the stones was paramount, and it was long before the mystic bond between the stone of the month, and the person born in that month was realised.

Nevertheless, nearly every book on gemstones will assign different stones for each month and Kunz himself, gives eight different listings from ancient Hebrew to the present day as examples. The following are taken from two contemporary publications on the subject — and even here, there are contradictions for the given stones against each month.

**Gemstones of the Month** (*Spells, Charms, Talismans & Amulets,* Pamela A Ball)

**January: Garnet, Onyx, Jet, Chrysoprase**
**February: Amethyst, Jasper, Rock crystal**
**March: Aquamarine, Bloodstone**
**April: Ruby, Garnet, Sard**
**May: Emerald, Malachite, Amber, Carnelian**
**June: Topaz, Agate, Alexandrite, Fluorite**

July: Moonstone, White agate
August: Cat's eye, Carnelian, Jasper, Fire agate
September: Peridot, Olivine, Chrysolite, Citrine
October: Opal, Tourmaline, Beryl, Turquoise
November: Topaz, Lapis lazuli
December: Serpentine, Jacinth, Peridot

**Gemstones of the Zodiac** (*Talismans, Charms & Amulets* Robert W. Wood)

**Aries** 21 March — 20 April **Red Jasper**
**Taurus** 21 April — 21 May **Rose Quartz**
**Gemini** 22 May — 21 June **Black Onyx**
**Cancer** 22 June — 22 July **Mother of Pearl**
**Leo** 23 July — 23 August **Tiger Eye**
**Virgo** 24 August — 22 September **Carnelian**
**Libra** 23 September — 23 October **Green Aventurine**
**Scorpio** 24 October — 22 November **Rhodonite**
**Sagittarius** 23 November — 21 December **Sodalite**
**Capricorn** 22 December — 20 January **Snowflake Obsidian**
**Aquarius** 21 January — 19$^t$ February **Blue Agate**
**Pisces** 20 February — 20 March **Amethyst**

When looking for authenticity in terms of magical working, however, there is an additional complication caused by historical calendar re-alignments and what is known as precession. Because of the tidal effects of the Sun and Moon, the Earth 'wobbles' like a spinning top, causing the direction of the vernal equinox to shift in the sky. The early calendar makers were unaware of this phenomenon and believed that in making the beginning of the year dependent on the Sun's entry into the constellation of Aries, they were fixing it forever to the time of the Winter Solstice. At that ancient point in time, **theoretically the gemstone representing Aries would have been that of the**

### *Winter Solstice*, i.e. December.

As the centuries rolled by, however, the stars of Aries receded from the Winter Solstice, moving steadily through almost a quarter of the great ecliptic and by the 2$^{nd}$ century BC, the Spring (or Vernal) Equinox was not far from the same point where the Winter Solstice had been when the first calendar-makers had fixed the constellation in the heavens. The Vernal Equinox is now on the cusp of Pisces and Aries but over the full 'wobble' it will move through all the signs in the zodiac — **at the moment the gemstone for Aries is represented by that of the *Vernal Equinox*, i.e. March.**

There is also some evidence in favour of the theory that at the outset all twelve stones were acquired by the same person and worn in turn, each one during the respective month to which it was assigned, or during the ascendancy of its zodiacal sign. According to the German writer Bruckmann (1773 *Abhandlung von Edelsteinen)*, "The stone of the month was believed to exercise its therapeutic (or magical) virtue to the fullest extent during that period. Perhaps the fact that this entailed a monthly change of ornaments may rather have been a recommendation of the usage than the reverse."

**When utilising gemstones as *magical* correspondences, however, it is vital that we use the *ancient* propensities for each stone ... because it is what the ancients believed, that locks *us* into the universal subconsciousness so quintessential for successful magic. We are talking here of esoteric archetypes not the fake-lore and fantasy of modern crystal working.**

The twelve stones of the High-Priest's breastplate — sardius (carnelian), topaz, carbuncle; emerald, sapphire (lapis lazuli), diamond (corundum or rock crystal); ligure (amber or jacinth), agate, amethyst; beryl, onyx, and jasper — set in four rows of three to signify the seasons as suggested by Flavii Josephi; and again by Clemens Alexandrius in the 2<sup>nd</sup> century, give us a starting point. Even then, things are not that simple. The c1539 edition of Marbodus's lapidary shows a figure of a High-Priest with the names and tribal attributions of the twelve stones, which differ slightly from the Greek Septuagint version from c250 BC as follows — and shows where the confusion over the inclusion of the sapphire may have arisen.

1.  Sardion (carnelian) — **Odem**
2.  Topazion (topaz) — **Pitdah**
3.  Smaragdus (carbuncle or emerald) — **Bareketh**
4.  Anthrax (carbuncle or emerald) — **Nophek**
5.  Sapphirus (lapis lazuli) — **Sappir**
6.  Iaspis (corundum) — **Yahalom**
7.  Ligurion (amber or jacinth — **Lesham**
8.  Achatâs (agate) — **Shebo**
9.  Amethystos (amethyst) — **Ahlamah**
10. Chrysolithos (beryl or chalcedony) — **Tarshish**
11. Beryllion (beryl or onyx) — **Shoham**
12. Onychion (green jasper) — **Yashpheh**

The above does not claim to be the earliest, authentic list since there is still the suggestion that the Hebrew system may have been based on the earlier Egyptian version. And, if at this point in history — before precession and calendar amendments interfered with the calculations — Aries as the first month of the ancient year would still have fallen around the time of the Winter Solstice.

Neither should we be dismissive of using an archaic Hebrew system as the foundation for our observances, for as any student of ritual magic will know, the Hebrew influence plays an important part in the development of the 'Western' system of the magical Qabalah and ritual magic.

## Art and Things ...

It was Aleister Crowley who taught that Magic was a blend of Art and Science, and so we should also be aware of the importance of magic crystals and sacred stones in the development of art. The colours of minerals are often striking and attractive; some colours only occur in certain minerals and these are consequently of great use to artists.

And while the lapidary in creating jewelled amulets or ornamenting precious reliquaries used most gemstones in the medieval period, some semi-precious varieties ended up on the artist's palette. In fact, artists and decorators have been using paints since prehistoric times, and until the 20$^{th}$ century, nearly all the colouring agents (pigments) they contained came from minerals. This was partly because the exact shades were unique and inimitable, and partly because colours that have been derived from minerals tend to be very stable, and do not fade in prolonged exposure to natural or artificial light.

As research into the nature of medieval pigments continues, azurite is recognised as a major source of the blues used by painters in the Middle Ages. Malachite was also widely used for bright green; ultramarine is an ancient pigment originally made from lapis lazuli; and vermilion came from cinnabar, a heavy opaque stone and the principal source of mercury. Zincite is known as 'Chinese white'; ochre, from the Greek *okhros* meaning 'pale yellow' and Sienna was used for a range of browns and orange-reds.

But it wasn't the experimental artists of the Middle Ages who first recognised the value of the stones beneath their feet. Fifteen thousand years after their creation, the paintings in the caves at Lascaux in south-western France and the Altamire cave in northern Spain still offer a spiritual window into the world of our prehistoric ancestors. Hundreds of images of animals brought to vibrant, immediate life on the walls — but these weren't the idle doodling of a bored caveman on a wet Late Stone Age afternoon, these were *sacred* images.

To create the paintings, these prehistoric artists obtained black from burning wood to make charcoal, and white from ground-up chalk. The weathering of most rocks will produce iron oxide, or haematite, a reddish-brown material that forms ochre, an iron-rich clay powder. Other natural minerals produced limonite (yellow and orange), magnetite (brown), or manganese oxide (dark brown). As Dr Stewart observes in *Journeys From the Centre of the Earth,* all they had to do was scrape it up from the ground, grind it into dust, mix it with some liquid, and paint it on. These early artists would have been experts at spotting that particular plants thrived on brownish and reddish soils and, scraping away the surface, found more colourful rocks — dazzling greens, brilliant blues and vibrant oranges. Painted far inside the cave's black interior, with no light apart from a primitive lamp of animal fat, the artist's work was no less sacred than the gaudy medieval frescos painted on the interior walls of our country churches.

And although marble is a crystalline carbonate rock formed by the metamorphism of limestone, it has been one of the world's most important materials for artistic expression — whether as the pink marble exterior of Milan Cathedral or the classical statues from ancient Greece. The name 'marble' derives from the Greek *marmairein,* meaning 'to gleam' in colours ranging from white or grey to a wide range of blacks, greens, pinks and reds.

- Gem-quality marble must have a consistent colouration and be resistant to abrasion.
- Marble for statuary must be pure white and have grains of a uniform size.
- Some coloured varieties of marble are also valuable: the most important are onyx marble (brown) and verd marble (green).

Marble is found all over the world and takes its pre-fix from the place from which it was quarried, or from its colour. For example: Connemara marble comes in colours from lime green to deep bottle green, and is flecked, banded and striated so there is a great deal of variation between individual pieces. Magically it is believed to be linked to "very deep and ancient energies, to a time when our ancestors could feel the flowing of Earth energies and the gods walked upon the earth" (*The Gemstones Handbook*).

As H. W. Janson observes in his *History of Art*, however, artistic creation is too subtle and intimate an experience to permit any precise analysis, and so it is difficult to draw a line between Art and Science and Magic. And much of what we see in the creation of these examples is a blend of artistic interpretation, based on the embryonic sciences of mineralogy and medicine, with a healthy dollop of magic (ritualised symbolism) thrown in for good measure.

Not only Art and Magic but also History has utilised gemstones as a form of symbolism. The heralds of the 17th century wanted to give additional importance to the 'science' of heraldry and invented the plan of emblazoning the arms of the nobility and royalty with the names of precious stones instead of using the ordinary terms for tinctures. (Tincture = the metals and colours used in heraldry. *Concise Encyclopaedia of Heraldry*, Guy Cadogan Rothery). For example:

Gold (Or) represented by a **topaz** and the Sun
Silver (Argent) represented by a **crystal** and the Moon
Red (Gules) represented by a **ruby** and Mars
Blue (Azure) represented by a **sapphire** and Jupiter
Black (Sable) represented by a **diamond** and Saturn
Green (Vert) represented by an **emerald** and Venus
Purple (Purpure) represented by an **amethyst** and Mercury

And from the ancient mythological concept of the bones of the

Earth Mother, we can see just how deeply magic crystals and sacred stones have permeated every aspect of human development throughout the ages.

## Try this exercise

In additional to your collection of natural stones and pebbles, begin to collect the twelve gemstones — polished or unpolished — one for each month or zodiacal sign. If using the stones listed in the Greek Septuagint version, green feldspar can be a substitute for emerald as this stone was listed for the 'breastplate of Aaron' and since these are all classed as *semi*-precious stones, they won't break the bank.

- Try to ensure that the gemstones in your collection are of a uniform size.

- Keep the astrological gemstones separate from the collection of natural stones by placing them in a special pouch especially chosen for the purpose.

- If purchasing any of the stones from a gem-shop or by mail order it is essential that they be thoroughly magically cleansed as they will have attracted all manner of negative energies whilst being handled by other people. Hold the stones cupped in the palms of your hands and hold under cold running water from the tap to purify them. Leave them on a clean white towel to dry naturally.

- Familiarise yourself with the magical correspondences for the astrological signs as an aid to divination. This will mean learning all the permutations of positive and negative aspects for each sign from a reputable book on astrology.

Make a point of carrying each of the gemstones about your person during the respective month to which it is assigned (or during the ascendancy of its zodiacal sign), in order to draw from its therapeutic or magical virtues to the fullest extent during that period.

# Chapter Six

# Black Sounds

From *Riches of the Earth*, we learn that during the Middle Ages, through the Renaissance and right up to the French Revolution, the royal banqueting tables had a curious item of tableware — the proving tree. This was a metal stand (often attached to the salt dish) that had from five to fifteen different 'stone' pendants hanging from its branches. These stones were believed to detect or neutralise poison in any of the foods or wines served during a meal, and it was the Chamberlain's job to dip the stones, one by one, into the food and wine as it was brought from the kitchen. Supposedly, the stones would sweat, change colour, or exhibit other reactions, if poison were present. And it might be a long time to wait before the King actually managed to eat his dinner!

Although proving trees were hung with precious stones (sapphires, rubies and emeralds), they also sported flints, agates, shark's teeth, toadstones (or borax), and bezoars. The toadstone was usually a piece of fossilised rock honeycombed with cavities that had been filled with deposits of carbonate of lime, although in medieval times such stones were believed to be hidden in the heads of toads, hence the name. Bezoars were composed of lime and magnesium but were not formed in the earth but as a concretion in the intestinal tracts of oriental deer and goats!

For thousands of years people have made up extraordinary stories about minerals and gemstones involving magic, astrology, alchemy and religious symbolism. According to *Treasures of the Earth*, although a large number of stones were accredited with the power to detect poison, many were also administered in cases of serious illness — the most impressive being the 'Most Noble Electuary of Jacinth'. This consisted of powdered jacinth (zircon), emerald, sapphire, topaz, pearl and red coral, with 22 other animal and vegetable ingredients; at times, the prescription was varied by adding white coral, amber, garnet and ruby to those already mentioned. A harmless but expensive and ineffectual cure was a paste of crushed pearls and lemon juice; although for sheer extravagance, few treatments can beat the 40,000 ducats of powdered gemstones administered to Pope Clement VII in 1534.

In fact, minerals and gemstones were believed to have healing properties that were every bit as curative as those of plants. Some gemstones were believed to calm fevers, cure hangovers and make warriors invisible; and sometimes scientific evidence supports the theories — Epsom salts really do clear out the digestive system. But other ideas, such as the belief that if you swallowed ground amethyst you could avoid a hangover, probably caused more internal bodily damage than a clear head. It is also unlikely that grinding agate and drinking it with wine would heal open wounds, or that sapphire mixed with milk would 'calm intestinal motions'.

The vast majority of these treatments were "simply expensive ways to accomplish nothing, or, what was worse, do the patient irreparable harm." Most were, of course, an outgrowth of sympathetic magic — such as applying red stones to inflamed or bleeding wounds, or topaz for jaundice, while the heliotrope (bloodstone) was applied to nosebleeds. Nevertheless, the attributes of the various different stones endured, and as an example, an 11th-century description in Old English of the magical virtues of the agate are identical to those given by Marbode and other earlier writers.

*Of the stone called agate it is said that it has eight virtues.*

*One is that when it thundereth it hurteth not the man that has this stone with him.*

*The second virtue is that in whatever house it be, therein may not a fiend be.*

*The third virtue is that no venom may hurt the man that has the stone with him.*

*The fourth virtue is that if the man that hath on him secretly the loathed fiend if he takes in water any fragments (gescearfenes) of this stone then is that soon made plain in him which before lay hid.*

*The fifth virtue is (that) he who is afflicted with any disease if he take that stone in water he is soon well.*

*The sixth virtue is that witchcraft hurteth not the man that hath it with him.*

*The seventh virtue is that he that taketh the stone in drink he hath the smoother body.*

*The eighth virtue of this stone is that no bite of snake kind may hurt him that tasteth the stone in water.*

In medieval Europe, lodestone (magnetite) was greatly valued for its therapeutic virtues. It is recorded that Trotula, the first of the female physicians connected with the celebrated School of Salerno, the centre of medical culture in Europe in the Middle Ages, recommended the use of lodestone in childbirth. It was also believed that wounds caused by burning could be healed if powdered lodestone were sprinkled over them. Ruptures, cured by first having a course of iron filings reduced to a fine powder, then a plaster made from crushed lodestone was applied externally, was a remedy that endured up until the 17<sup>th</sup> century.

The therapeutic effects were often sought and found in some association between the colour of the stone and the malady or infirmity to be cured — similar to the Doctrine of Signatures in plants. For example:

- **Yellow stones** were supposed to be beneficial to sufferers of jaundice.

- **Red stones** were endowed with the power of checking the flow of blood. The bloodstone was prescribed because by its mere touch, it could stem the most violent of haemor-rhages.

- **Green stones** were regarded as beneficial for sight, and the emerald and other green stones were said to have great curative powers for the eyes.

- **White or clear stones** were associated with the moon and supposed to have the power to conjure evil influences and to drive away the powers of darkness.

Although our modern perceptions about the 'placebo effect' makes us sceptical about these medieval cures, from a magical perspective we still need to understand these dubious correspondences!

## The Power of Elixirs

From the 15$^{th}$ century, the steeping of stones in fluids so that their power might be imbibed, bound to, or suspended over the patient's body, became a popular cure. A medical work for the time, the *Hortus Sanitatis*, lists 144 stones and the means of using them medicinally, although the *Ebers Papyrus* (c1500 BC but copied from a manuscript of c3000 BC) has lapis lazuli and hematite among its curative substances. Theophrastus, a student of Aristotle wrote a book on gems and some of their medical uses in the 3$^{rd}$ century BC, as did the Greek pharmacist Dioscorides, and the Roman encyclopaedist Pliny in the 1st century AD. Hildegarde of Bingen (12$^{th}$ century) continued the tradition, which lasted to the 18$^{th}$ century when many of the stones were still listed in the pharmacopoeias of the day.

Following the Greek tradition, the stones were administered internally, and as extensive as the medicinal and physical properties of stones were (whether real or imagined), their magical uses equalled them. Amulets, for example, were protective devices worn around the body, or placed next to other objects, to protect them from various evils of the body or mind.

We should not forget that these beliefs were common in all societies during all periods of antiquity, and their use was accepted as normal by secular, religious and the 'scientific' authorities of the day (i.e. the physicians). Almost anything could serve as an amulet: it could be prepared at home, and required no specific knowledge or magical skills. Given their mundane nature, such amulets are often hard to identify — for when we come across an unusual stone, how can we tell whether it was an amulet, or merely a piece of decorative ornament?

Today, gem elixirs are often recommended by psychics in order to help restore the healthy energy of the body and for their curative powers; Edgar Cayce, the American psychic, often suggested gem drinks. To make an elixir, it requires the correct gem, unpolished, uncut, in crystal form if possible, and clean — then placed in sunshine to activate its healing powers.

According to Eva Shaw in *Book of Divining the Future*, the querent would sit in a quiet place to meditate. After a few moments, the gem is put in the centre of a clear glass bowl; the bowl is filled with distilled water and covered with a piece of glass to keep the elixir clean. The bowl should be left on a natural surface such as wood or glass, and preferably in the sunshine for about two hours, after which the liquid should be stored in a tightly sealed glass bottle, or consumed immediately.

Chrissie Semper's *Gemstones Handbook* offers a slightly different and more modern approach in that she uses super-market spring water or rainwater, and places the container out of doors "where the light of the full moon, or clear sunlight can shine on it for a total of three hours." Pour the liquid into a dark glass bottle, topping up half and half with brandy (as a preserv-ative); shake vigorously for 30 seconds and then place in a dark cupboard until required. By rule of thumb, stones with sun properties will affect physical well-being, and moon elixirs would work on the spiritual, psychic or metaphysical planes.

The most commonly used elixirs are:

- **Amethyst** for calming the disposition and reducing stress.
- **Bloodstone** for improvement of any bone marrow condition, and the health of testicles, ovaries, cervix and uterus.
- **Citrine** to reduce and /or remove toxins from the legs and feet.
- **Diamond** to remove any blockages and pockets of negativity, anxiety and insecurity.
- **Jade** to improve a balance in the mind and the body to increase wisdom, psychic abilities and promote courage.
- **Onyx** to help restore the heart, kidneys and nerve tissues of the body.
- **Rose quartz** to assist the body in reducing emotional disruptions and providing a feeling of balance and self-confidence.
- **Turquoise** is the 'master healer' since it moves through the body quickly, strengthening and regenerating it, while protecting the colours of the aura.

Like a lot of cures, the success of the treatment is also reliant on the belief in the 'placebo effect' — a cure given to humour or gratify a patient rather than to exercise any physically curative effect.

## The Essence of the Stones

Nevertheless, there is a powerful and widespread occult belief that everything on the planet, both animate and inanimate, has a life force of its own. As already discussed, stones are known to attract and hold psychic energies, and the following stories will demonstrate how ordinary stones can retain the 'essence of spirit' of their original place.

## A Stone from the Mesa Verde

"Many years ago a friend visiting the Mesa Verde National Park located in Montezuma County, Colorado, brought back a small piece of sandstone from the ruins built by the ancestral Puebloan people between 550 to 1300 AD. The site, which is Spanish for 'green table', is best known for its cliff dwellings, which are structures built within caves and under outcropping in cliffs. The stone was an ordinary piece of sandstone, picked up from the Mesa floor, without any distinguishing features or markings — except that it carried with it an extremely powerful aura of a dusty arid land.

The stone was put away in a drawer with a collection of joss sticks, etc., and not seen again for some five or six years prior to a house move. Whereas everything else in the drawer was permeated with the strong scent of the joss, the sandstone had retained its own distinctive smell of a baking hot, sun-bleached landscape that had not lessened over the years.

Although no-one else wanted it, it was felt that it would be wrong to just cast it out into an alien landscape, and the decision was taken to return the sandstone to the land of its creation when other friends were due to visit Colorado later in the year. It may seem strange to say that such a small piece of rock could exude such a strong 'presence', and although there was nothing sinister or uncomfortable about it, the stone just felt out of sinc with *our* native landscape."

## Stone from the Mediterranean.

"I brought back a granite worry stone from the beach at Menton in the South of France. The surface is speckled with individual mineral grains that sparkle in the sunlight and it is just large enough to sit comfortably in the palm of the hand. There is nothing left of the original smell of the sea but it creates a wonderful calming effect when rolled gently between the palms of my hands.

It was one of those holidays when everything was perfect and thirty years later, the stone still conjures up the feeling of complete relaxation and an absence of stress. It's thought-association I suppose but the stone seems to exude the tranquillity and harmony of a gently rolling sea."

## Try this exercise

Unlike the medicinal ground gemstones, an elixir made from a crystal preparation isn't going to cause any damage but if we are experimenting with the power of magic crystals and sacred stones, we need to experience some of the 'cures' recommended by magicians and alchemists from the past.

## Elixir preparation

Select one of the methods given in this chapter under elixirs and make the preparation as directed. For the purpose of the experiment, chose one of the following gemstones according to the results you wish to achieve.

- **Amethyst** for calming the disposition and reducing stress.

- **Jade** to improve a balance in the mind and the body to increase wisdom, psychic abilities and promote courage.

- **Rose quartz** to assist the body in reducing emotional disruptions and providing a feeling of balance and self-confidence.

Once the preparation is ready, drink a small wine glass of the elixir for three successive days and see whether you think there is any reduction in your stress levels or increase in your psychic abilities. Keep a record of the experiment in your magical journal.

**It should be noted that elixirs do not replace medical treatment. For any health concerns, professional medical advice is always recommended.**

Chapter Seven

# Slow Fires of Autumn

For all the great wealth and benefits derived from the riches of the Earth, however, many of the minerals can have some unpleasant, if not dangerous effects. In ancient times metals like mercury and arsenic *were* famed for their lethal potential but lead, for instance is such a deadly, insidious poison that its continuous use has been given as a plausible reason for the 'slow and complicated demise' of the Roman Empire. The fire-retardant properties of asbestos were also known to the Greeks, who were in awe of a stone that could be woven but not destroyed by fire, and gave it the name *asvestos*, meaning inextinguishable. Throughout ancient history, it was thought of as a substance of almost magical properties.

As we discussed in Chapter Two, regardless of where we live in the world, ancient sites reveals where our indigenous ancestors located the power-places that were to become the focus of subsequent religious beliefs. We now know that the most important aspect of each site was not what was seen above ground, but what influenced by the geological formations beneath their feet.

## Earth Energies

There is a train of thought, especially those of contemporary pagan belief, that *any* energy that comes from the Earth is automatically beneficial; and that because they embrace the Earth on a spiritual level they have nothing to fear from it. Let's make no bones about it: some of the effects of earth energies upon humans can have a devastating outcome. The rocks and minerals beneath our feet can give off all manner of emissions

In *What You Call Time*, the author, Suzanne Ruthven, observes that when referring to 'earth mysteries', it is necessary to understand the difference between a 'place of power' and a sacred site. For example, a large number of modern pagans treat ancient earthworks as either power places or sacred sites, without any thought of the religious antecedents. But as one magical practitioner pointed out, such activities are on a par with worshipping at a castle moat or Neolithic flint quarry! Simply because something is old does not mean it has, or had, a religious or ritual usage.

> *"In human terms, a power site may have been as mundane as the boundary between two neighbouring peoples. Such places became endowed with the appellation 'powerful' and, through time, assigned deities and genus loci (spirit of place) thereby becoming in our eyes holy — sacred. Not only would they become sacred but eventually sacred to a particular god/dess. That is to say, set aside for the use of the deity, or a place where, should the god be so inclined, the individual might be blessed with a visitation. Alternatively they could be blasted by them or the natural forces they control — human presence is not always welcome at some sites of power."* (What You Call Time)

By comparison, and equally as important, are the massive stone formations found on the American northern Plains, known as medicine wheels. According to Alvin M. Josephy in *500 Nations*, the medicine wheels were constructed with "piles of rocks laid out on the ground in a pattern of concentric circles or ovals intersected by spokes radiating out from a central cairn." Archaeologists suggest that these strange rock formations, some a hundred feet in diameter, were used by the Plains people for religious purposes as well an annual calendar and maps. Most of the medicine wheels are located on elevated sites with the spokes pointing out "toward major landmarks and toward other medicine wheels on far-off peaks." The Native American has a culture that goes back thousands of years and today's Plain's people still consider them to be sacred. As Josephy observes, it is hard to imagine otherwise: "In their silence and timelessness, the medicine wheels have connected people with the supernatural, the land, and with one another through uncounted generations."

What we must realise, is that power-sites become sacred by a dedicated usage while other places may have been consecrated for a specific religious purpose. The construction of the West Kennet (Wiltshire) and New Grange (Ireland) burial sites are prime examples. Rituals held in the past would have been purely dedicated to the cult of ancestor worship and *possibly* the deities concerned with death and rebirth. It seems unlikely that such sites would have been visited for anything other than those rites for which they were designed, but they would have been originally chosen because of the natural energies associated with that particular site. Another magical practitioner, however, had a warning tale to tell:

*"A couple of my acquaintance decided to work a ritual at an ancient site in the hope that they would have a child. Unfortunately, the place they chose was a burial site and during the following two years, they lost four babies through miscarriage. Coincidence? Maybe, but if we consider the generations of 'magical' overlay on the site and the deities to whom the souls of the dead may have been commended, I for one, am not surprised at the tragic outcome. I also believe that if they had no other alternative than to work there, they may have stood a better chance if they had re-worded their ritual to include such things as 'gateway to a new physical life'."* (What You Call Time)

It is not always necessary to go to the actual power centre of Glastonbury, Avebury or Stonehenge to draw upon earth energies since accessibility and a lack of privacy could make working difficult; some of these principal sites, as previous suggested, may have been corrupted by the tramp of generations of sight-seeing and tourism. Using an Ordnance Survey map to locate the ancient/natural/historic sites; draw a straight line from the main site to any other place where there are the remains of ancient worship, and anywhere along that line will be good for tapping into earth energy. Dion Fortune explained that the lines of force *between* the power centres serve a better purpose as the magical Adept can access quite enough power without being overwhelmed by it. Standing stones trace these power lines on high ground while hammer-pools are located on low ground "because water shows up in a valley bottom among trees, where stones wouldn't to get a dead straight line across country."

Next to Stonehenge, the next most famous site must be Glastonbury, a place so steeped in myth and legend that the very name conjures up the mists and mystery. Even by Celtic times, Glastonbury was known as a strange place — an entrance to the Otherworld — and it is from Celtic bards that the mysteries of the Tor have survived. But the mysteries of Glastonbury are not confined to myth, and the Celts themselves were no strangers to Otherworldlyness. There are the very obvious physical sensations that can afflict those climbing the Tor, while local weather conditions produce some extremely weird phenomena. According to Robin Ellis ('Dreams of Avalon' an article published in *Phoenix* magazine), there is a long tradition that some immense power lies hidden deep within the Tor. Some believe it to exist deep within a Crystalline Cave that lies behind a sealed entrance close to the Blue Pool; while the sacredness of the site is also suggested by the excavated remains of yew trees, dating back to the Iron Age. With such an excess of psychic energy on tap, discipline should be the watch-word of anyone attempting a magical operation at any sacred site:

*"Anyone who intends using Earth energies for 'negative' purposes*

*should be very wary," came the warning. "This isn't simple moralising. Any magical intention which is based on a negative emotion such as greed, envy or hate is an aspect of impurity within ourselves — we all have such thoughts and feelings, it's giving them expression which can be dangerous — and aiming to channel such strong negative energies through these natural power lines ... Well, let's hope that the operation simply fails, as the consequences could be seriously disturbing at the very least."*

Many magical practitioners believe that sacred sites have their own 'guardians' to prevent amateurs making improper use of site-energies. In *Needles of Stone*, Tom Graves cites the group of students who acquired a *grimoire* (spell book) and decided to perform a magical working on top of an ancient earth barrow at night — for a joke. Whatever happened spooked the group so badly that they panicked and ran. For some time afterwards, the students were plagued by the fear of being stalked, some even requiring psychiatric counselling before they were able to overcome the fear of being followed.

According to Graves it was impossible to get an exact description of what suddenly appeared on top of the barrow, as its appearance was slightly different for each of the students involved but as any magical Adept would realise, this is a characteristic of 'guardians' and many other kinds of elemental earth energy. This is not the 'black magic' of fictional horror stories; no demons being conjured up from the Abyss. It is merely a natural safety valve to stop inexperienced or foolish people from coming into contact with forces they cannot control or understand, as demonstrated on a visit to Castlerigg stone circle, when occult author, Aeron Medbh-Mara, took the opportunity to chat to other visitors about why they were there:

*"With only one exception the answer was 'Because it's a sacred site'. When questioned further not one could explain to whom it*

*was sacred nor why. Nevertheless they still all agreed that it was an impressive ring of stones set in beautiful countryside, and that they had a feeling that an undefined 'something' should happen to them while they were there."*

But even if we think that all this is psychic wishful thinking let's look at the most famous power-place of the ancient world — Delphi. This was an oracular shrine of Apollo in his temple at Delphi, where the priestess of the god (called the Pythia), seated on a tripod over a fissure in the rock "uttered in divine ecstacy incoherent words" (*The Oxford Companion to Classical Literature*) in reply to the questions of the suppliants. This 'divine ecstacy' was caused by vapors rising up from a chasm in the rock, and recent geological investigations have shown that gas emissions from a geologic chasm in the earth *could* have inspired the Pythia to 'connect with the divine'. Some researchers suggest the possibility that methane might have been the gas emitted from the chasm, and that the chasm itself might have been a seismic rupture. Delphi was also considered to be the 'navel of the world', marked by an *omphalos*, an ancient religious stone artifact: a round sacred stone said to have been flung to earth by Zeus.

And if the most famous power-place in the ancient world can be partially explained as being the result of seismic activity, can other power-places recognised as such by the ancients, also be the result of similar phenomena? Earth energies appear to be pockets of natural intensity, such as black springs and underground streams, that certain 'gifted' people can draw upon and harnessed for various purposes. This 'gift' is frequently looked upon as being both 'blessing and curse' since the bearer has limited control over the receiving of such psychic sensations, which seem to be stronger when in close proximity to these natural pockets. Non-psychic people, however, can still be afflicted by headaches and feelings of being agitated and confused.

## Ley Lines and *The Old Straight Track*

Anyone who is fascinated by the subject of ley-lines will have a copy of Alfred Watkins's *The Old Straight Track*. First published in 1925, it caused violent controversy in archaeological circles due to the fact that Watkins claimed to have identified an ancient system of straight tracks (or leys) that criss-crossed the British Isles and which were old when the Romans came to Britain. First in his native Herefordshire, and later across the entire British countryside, Watkins noticed that beacon hills, mounds, earthworks, moats and old churches built on pagan sites seemed to follow straight lines.

The concept of ley lines is generally thought of solely in relation to Watkins, but there were several other similar theories going around at the time, mainly those attributed to English astronomer, Norman Lockyer. In June 1921, Watkins had gone riding near some hills in the vicinity of Bredwardine, when he noticed that many of the footpaths appeared to connect one hilltop to another in a straight line. He was studying a map when he noticed the alignment, and the whole thing came to him in a flash. It has also been suggested that Watkins's insight was also influenced by an account by William Henry Black given to the British Archaeological Association, titled *Boundaries and Landmarks*, in which he had speculated that "monuments exist marking grand geometrical lines which cover the whole of Western Europe."

Watkins theorised that, in ancient times, when Britain was far more densely forested, the country was criss-crossed by a network of straight-line travel routes, with prominent features of the landscape being used as navigational points. His work also cited a paper by a G. H. Piper (1882), which noted that "A line drawn from the Skirrid-fawr mountain northwards to Arthur's Stone would pass over the camp and southern most point of Hatterall Hill, Oldcastle, Longtown Castle, and Urishay and Snodhill castles."

Watkins's lengthy investigations subsequently alleged that the British Isles were covered by a vast web of straight tracks, aligned with either the sun or the path of a star. Ley lines and earth energies can't be scientifically defined because, as those who work with them have discovered, the energy-flow waxes and wanes. They can even change polarity, ebbing and flowing like the tides; they may even change character with the seasons:

*"To complicate things even further, our own perception of these energies can change and colour them, influenced by such things as our current state of mind, our convictions and beliefs, and even the weather! It's not surprising that the hardened sceptic experiences no revelation in a stone circle,"* explains an adherent of Earth Mysteries. *"The perception of earth energies is unique to each observer. At sacred sites there is an abundance of 'energy' available, to reinforce whatever views and strongly held beliefs we may unconsciously use to channel those energies through."*

Watkins theorized that these alignments were created for ease of overland trekking by line of sight navigation during Neolithic times and had persisted in the landscape over millennia incorporating a number of places of geographical interest, such as ancient monuments and megaliths, natural ridge-tops and waterfords. In more recent times, the term 'ley lines' has come to be associated with spiritual and mystical theories about land forms, including Chinese feng shui and Earth Mysteries. In 2004, John Bruno Hare wrote:

*"Watkins never attributed any supernatural significance to leys; he believed that they were simply pathways that had been used for trade or ceremonial purposes, very ancient in origin, possibly dating back to the Neolithic, certainly pre-Roman. His obsession with leys was a natural outgrowth of his interest in landscape photography and love of the British countryside. He was an*

*intensely rational person with an active intellect, and I think he would be a bit disappointed with some of the fringe aspects of ley lines today."*

Again, we are forced to examine this sacred geometry of the landscape and try to find the common ground where contemporary romance, science and ancient wisdom are compatible. Nevertheless, there are those who can plug-in to certain psychic sensations when in close proximity to leys, while others experience a sudden feeling of agitation and disorientation for no apparent reason

## The Unsung Pioneer

Thomas Charles Lethbridge was a British explorer, archaeologist and parapsychologist, educated at Wellington College, before attending Trinity College, Cambridge, where he discovered an interest in archaeology. Having completed his degree, he began working as a voluntary digger for the curator of the Archaeological Museum in Cambridge: although he had a private income, Lethbridge became the keeper of Anglo-Saxon antiquities at the museum.

He was a dedicated researcher who considered occult phenomena with what he considered to be a scientific approach and put forward theories on ghosts, witchcraft, dowsing and psychokinesis. *The Power of the Pendulum*, documents his research into dowsing by means of the pendulum, but he died while the manuscript was still in draft form. The book is a conclusion to the author's lifelong study of the worlds of the unexplained and the occult. Through his experience with the pendulum and his work with dreams, Lethbridge concluded that there are other realms of reality beyond this one and that the soul is probably immortal.

There is a theory that an ebbing and flowing energy current moves through the earth and that some people experience 'shocks' when touching standing stones — although not everyone can feel them, and they are not always present. Lethbridge wrote widely on his experiments with dowsing by the use of a pendulum and recorded an instance of this kind at the Merry Maidens stone circle in Cornwall:

*"As soon as the pendulum started to swing, a strange thing happened. The hand resting on the stone received a strong tingling sensation like a mild electric shock and the pendulum itself shot out until it was circling nearly horizontally to the ground. The stone itself, which must have weighed over a ton, felt as if it were rocking and dancing about ... The next day I sent my wife up alone to see what happened to her. She had the same experience."*

Regardless of the object suspended, the pendulum should have a special significance for each individual dowser, suggests Eva Shaw in *The Book of Divining the Future*, and this often a crystal or gemstone. Surprisingly enough, pendulums are still widely used in the location of hidden objects and to uncover natural resources such as water and minerals. The dowser generally walks around the area with the pendulum suspended from a chain, thread or cord, while concentrating on what is to be located — when contact is made, the pendulum swings (see the exercise at the end of Chapter Four of *Magic Crystals, Sacred Stones*).

The pendulum will also pick up on underground streams, and what are called 'black' or 'blind springs'– underground fissures that allow currents of energy to seep up from deep within the earth. These are often the site of ghostly apparitions and other psychic phenomena, and the pendulum is the means of identifying the source of such happenings in the case of any adverse effects, such as any unpleasant poltergeist manifestations, suspected hauntings, peculiar sensations, etc.

## The Silent Killers

Not all earth energies or mineral emissions, manifest on a psychic level. Aluminium, cadmium, chromium, copper molybdenum, nickel and zinc are toxic, as are antimony, selenium, thallium and silver. Ironically, the trace elements most essential for our health are chromium, cobalt, fluorine, iodine, iron, manganese, molybdenum, selenium and zinc! In small quantities, they may do us good, but in larger amounts, the bones of the Earth Mother *can* cause considerable harm.

## The Decline of the Roman Empire

According to *Journeys From the Centre of the Earth*, in the frozen wastes of Greenland, in ice layers dating back thousands of years, lead particles are barely detectable in pre-history. These ice cores reveal that lead concentrations started to rise around 8,000 years ago when the Mesopotamians began using lead-smelting furnaces; soared dramatically around 600 BC when the Greeks started lead mining on a massive scale; and peaked around the end of the 1$^{st}$ century BC during the Roman Empire.

We know now that lead is not a human-friendly metal, but the Romans couldn't get enough of it — they used it to line their aqueducts, in mortar in stone structures, for public and domestic plumbing. The sheer volume of fresh water flowing through the pipes and cisterns probably prevented ordinary citizens from ingesting too much lead, but it is a cumulative poison and its most serious effects may not appear for decades.

Upper class Romans, however, were much more exposed and a large amount of their food was laden with lead. To stop their wines turning sour during shipment, they prepared a preservative called *sapa*, a concoction made from unfermented grape juice boiled in a lead kettle. In fact, nearly 20 per cent of the dishes in a typical Roman recipe book have this dark, sweet aromatic syrup used as a sweetening agent — and it was highly toxic.

Dr Iain Stewart also points out that some scientists have suggested that the high lead content might have contributed to the start of the slow and complicated demise of the Roman Empire. History tells us that from the 1st century AD, the Roman upper classes suffered from the inability to reproduce — a prominent symptom of lead poisoning. They began to die out with extreme rapidity, while the health and mental capacity of the emperors appeared to decline among the successors to Augustus, several succumbing to illness and erratic behaviour. As Dr Stewart observes — the ice cores indicate that lead levels in the atmosphere began to plummet around the end of the 1st century AD as the Roman lead mines became exhausted and closed — but perhaps the damage had already been done to the Imperial Roman world.

## Radioactive Time Bomb

The use of lead may have been curtailed but there is another killer on the prowl that appears to be a growing problem in the 21st century — radon. Radon is formed as part of the normal radioactive decay chain of uranium and thorium, both of which have been around since the earth was formed. Their most common isotope has a very long half-life (4.5 billion years), and will continue to occur for millions of years at about the same concentrations as it does now.

Radon is responsible for the majority of public exposure to ionizing radiation, and often the single largest contributor to an individual's background radiation dose, which varies from location to location. Radon gas from natural sources can accumulate in buildings, especially in confined areas such as attics and basements. It can also be found in some spring water and hot springs, with geological conditions in certain areas leading to higher than average levels.

Medical studies have shown a clear link between breathing high concentrations of radon and incidence of lung cancer, with radon being considered a significant contaminant that affects indoor air quality worldwide. According to the United States Environmental Protection Agency, for example, radon is the second most frequent cause of lung cancer, after cigarette smoking, causing 21,000 lung cancer deaths per year in North America.

Reflecting on the fact that no matter how spiritually minded or eco-friendly we consider ourselves to be, it counts for nothing in the grander scheme of things. In an article entitled 'The Pathway of Nuit' published in *Phoenix* magazine, Dr Mériém Clay-Egerton took a far more brutal and far-reaching view of humanity and its feeble attempts to harmonise with the Earth:

The planet is shaking itself free, initially to try and eradicate the parasites which are disturbing it ... All that homo sapiens could have produced now bucks, wavers and breaks down, and will finally disappear. It is no longer a bright and proud future, but dark and sullen. The Earth realises that to free herself she must destroy herself and start again with new building bricks. But she can't tell the guilty from the innocent, so all will go, as they must, into infinity. The great pool of chaos.

In the future, if there is any future to come — if this environmental niché has not been blown apart or torn to pieces by the so-called dominant animal species — what would an archaeologist find to say about us? Would he consider homo sapiens to be a worthy holder of the planet? Or would he be a noisome evil, spreading blight — a parasite upon the planet's surface? In all charity he would see him as a dead end: unable to progress further; totally unable to comprehend what had happened to his world.

Our present day archaeologists looks this way at homo neanderthalensis, dubbing him as too primitive — in fact, subnormal! Only fit to be superseded by a newer, more intelligent species. It's modern man who's lost his roots. Unable to listen to the planet that bore him, he has total incomprehension of the silence that could give him new insights into his future.

Among our magic crystals and sacred stones, for all their great worth, and the benefits derived from the riches of the Earth, many really do have a some very unpleasant, if not dangerous effects.

## Try this exercise:

White stones have always been seen as having a magical or mystical use within traditional witchcraft, and the burying of white stones or lumps of quartz with the dead was customary in early times.

- In Ireland, white stones were believed to have the power of revealing enemies and mischief-makers. Drop a white pebble into clear water (i.e. a shallow stream) and the culprit's face will appear. At home, use a dark bowl filled with water.

- Naturally white stones are prized for their luck, or for their curative powers. When finding a small white stone it should be spat on and then thrown over your head, saying *Luck, lucky stone. Bring me luck when I go home.* It is important not to look back when turning round a corner.

- White quartz can often be found in the most unusual shapes (i.e. a hound's tooth, pyramid, etc) and these should be kept separate for divination purposes.
- Days marked with a white stone were said to be days of pleasure, and to be remembered with gratification. Where possible keep a white stone found on this day for future

use in divination, or purely as a souvenir.

The famous Scottish amulet of white quartz owned by the chiefs of Clan Donnachaidh, and known as the Stone of the Banner, was looked upon as a powerful talisman in battle ... water in which it had been dipped was said to cure disease.

# Chapter Eight

# To the Dark Wood

Rocks are made from minerals, and hundreds of minerals, in differing amounts make up hundreds of different kinds of rock. Some are formed from hot watery solutions inside the Earth, forming when heat deep inside the Earth melts minerals in the rocks, which later cool and harden into what we know as crystals. But minerals aren't just found in rocks; some, usually referred to as 'organic minerals', come from plants and animals, and include coal, jet, coral, amber and pearls.

## Amber

Amber is formed from the compressed and impacted resin of coniferous trees and one of the first 'gems' to be used by primitive man for grave goods and decoration; employed at this very early stage for amulets and medical purposes — rough, worked amber being found in deposits from the Stone Age. At one time, amber was said to be the solidified urine of the lynx (one of its names was *lyncurius*) and as such, represented the Sun and its animal correspondence.

That amber would acquire a charge of static electricity when rubbed with a cloth was recorded as early as 600 BC by the Ionic philosopher, Thales, and from his observation may be dated the beginning of the study of electrical phenomena. It was classified as a firestone and believed to offer protection against fire and water; it was also thought to give courage and sometimes presented to Roman gladiators before they entered the arena to fight.

Medicinally it was thought to have therapeutic properties in the treatment of diseases of the respiratory tract and nervous disability. It helped in dispersing negative energy and to speed self-healing; and was a particular safeguard for unborn babies. It was also credited with being able to detect poison by some change in the clearness or colour and highly valued, especially red amber, carried as an amulet to protect against poison, ill health, and the Evil Eye.

Magically, amber is worn by witches as a badge of rank and if the piece contains the fossilised remains of plants or insects that lived millions of years ago, so much the better. Those who have acquired a piece of amber so mysteriously formed by Nature's hand, probably feel that they have indeed obtained a talisman of great power.

## Coal

Coal is what we call a 'fossil fuel' — a source of energy derived from the decomposition of trees and other plants. This vegetable matter has fallen to the ground and been compressed by subsequent layers of soil and further deposits of the same type. This sequence, repeated over and over again, created the great coal deposits of the Upper Carboniferous period in Britain.

Coal and anthracite occasionally shows evidence of its origins in the form of plant fossils, such as the imprints of leaves. Most of that mined today was formed more than 280 million years ago, when the earth was covered by luxuriant forests, including huge trees, giant ferns, mosses and horsetails that grew in giant swamps. Many of the coal seams formed during this period are not especially thick and are separated by other strata, such as sandstones and mudstones. These inorganic rocks were formed when water covered the land and plant growth ceased for a while.

Medicinally, its main uses derived from the tar acids such as salicylic acid, nitro phenol and picric acid; some medicines are also obtained from benzol, which comes from light oil. Medicine made from salicylic acid/coal tar/sulphur is used in the treatment of scaly skin disorders of the scalp such as psoriasis, eczema, seborrhoeic dermatitis and dandruff. Sulphur is an antiseptic and also helps break down skin scales. Magically, coal represents Time and can often be found fashioned into small figures that can be used as amulets. Sea coal can be found washed up on the beach and, heavily impregnated with salt water, it burns with the most amazing colours.

## Coral

Coral is an animal gemstone that is made from the skeletal remains of sea creatures called coral polyps. Coral grows by extracting dissolved carbonate salts from the surrounding water and converting them into a hard protective shell. There are two main varieties:

- The blue, pink, red and white are composed mainly of calcium carbonate. Red coral is the most valuable and widely used in jewellery; blue coral is the rarest.

- The black or golden species are formed from a horn-like substance called conchiolin.

According to George Frederick Kunz, coral has been classed as a precious stone for 20 centuries and to render its wearer any service, it must have been freshly gathered from the sea, or have been cast up by the sea on the shore. Medicinally, coral was believed to staunch the flow of blood from a wound, cure madness, and give wisdom to the wearer. Children were given coral beads to wear for protection, and it was used as an antidote against poison.

Magically, red or white coral was said to still tempests and allow the wearer to traverse broad rivers in safety. It was carried as a protection against the Evil Eye, curses and negative thinking, although if it is accidentally broken, the separate pieces have no magical /protective virtue, and the magic power ceases in the main piece "as though the spirit dwelling in the coral had fled from its abode."

## Fossils

Hidden away among the rocks found in the Earth's crust, are the beautiful preserved remains of creatures and plants that existed in bygone geological ages. It is now generally accepted that a fossil is a remnant, impression or trace of an animal or plant that has been recognisably preserved in the Earth's crust and dating back more than 2500 million years. Generally speaking, it is mainly the bones, teeth, shells and wood that become fossilised, and each fossil will be the same age as the stratum of rock in which it lies.

Fossils are formed from the petrified remains of these plants or animals, which millions of years ago, sank into the mud beneath the sea or was quickly buried following an earthquake, volcanic eruption, avalanche or sandstorm. The remains were turned to stone as silica filtered into the space occupied by the decaying organism to leave a hard, mineralised replica in its place. Fossils may also be the petrified impressions or casts of plants and boneless animals — such as algae or jellyfish — whose tissues have decomposed.

George Kunz tells the story of a remarkable find in the Australian opal-fields in 1909: a reptilian skeleton resembling a small snake that had become opalised by natural processes. A specimen of Nature's handiwork possessing a beauty exceeding that to be found in any work of man, he wrote, "As an amulet in ancient times it would have been valued at an immense sum, for the figure of a serpent was a favourite symbol … especially to all those who are interested in occult science, and all who appreciate the poetic and perhaps mystic significance of form, sign and symbol." Medicinally, fossils have no known use but magically they can be used as amulets for longevity and endurance.

## Ivory

Ivory has been prized by humans since the earliest times because of its beautiful colouration and fine texture. It is both extremely hard wearing and very easy to carve. The oldest known carved ivory was found in France: it was taken from the tusk of a mammoth and is thought to be more than 30,000 years old. Ivory was also widely used in ancient Egypt for jewellery and amulets.

Medicinally, the demand for ivory is largely for use in Chinese medicine although it has very little medical value apart from the placebo effect. Magically, ivory is used to draw wealth and power but any item that comes into our possession will be old since the killing of ivory-bearing animals is now outlawed internationally, and the supply of new ivory has almost ceased. If a piece does come into our hands, rather than being repelled by the idea of owning an ivory object, we should look upon it as a sacred trust. This was once part of a living creature, and that part of its spirit lives on, in the guise of a rare and precious amulet.

## Jet

Jet is formed from wood that has fallen into water and become compacted into a hard and durable gemstone: unlike other types of coal, which form on land, it is found in rocks of marine origin. Jet has been found among Palaeolithic remains and from very early times was already regarded as having certain talismanic virtues. "Such ornaments were believed to become part of the very body and soul of the wearer, and were therefore to be guarded with jealous care" (Dr Moriz Hoernes *Urgeschichte der bildenden Kunst*, 1898).

Jet is a black, fine-grained variety of coal, which can be cut and shaped into jewellery and other decorative objects. It is either black lignite or cannel coal, a variety formed mostly from plant seeds, spores, algae and fungal material, which can spontaneously combust after having been dampened. This was the stone referred to in the late medieval *Hortus Sanitatis*, that was said to catch fire when water was thrown on it, but which could be extinguished by oil!

Medicinally, it was generally set on fire for purposes of suffumigation, to bring on the menses, as well as for another common medieval ailment, epilepsy. Dropsy was cured by this means, as was indigestion; and as a water solution, it was a sure way to fasten loose teeth in the gums; as an aid a difficult birth and could be used to verify virginity. Magically, burning jet drove away snakes and demons, dissolving the wicked spells of magicians and all deceitful illusions and prophesies of evil omen. It has been included in the funerary rites from Neolithic times, and was widely used for jewellery in Victorian Britain when people went into mourning.

## Keratin (Horn)

Horn is a general term that describes a wide range of antlers and similar protuberances from a wide variety of animals, including birds, insects and lizards. Scientifically, however, a true horn can only be a core of bone surrounded by a layer of keratin found in a certain species of buffalo and rhinoceros.

Medicinally, horn (and particularly rhino-horn) plays an important part in traditional Chinese medicine where the horn in powdered form is used as an aphrodisiac. Horn was also believed to detect poison and protect from epilepsy. Magically and traditionally, a ram's horn and deer antlers are a symbol of virility, and can be obtained naturally, especially antlers, which are shed each year.

## Meteorite

In strict scientific terms, the word 'meteor' should only be applied to small chunks of stony or metallic matter for as long as they remain in outer space. When they are drawn into the Earth's upper atmosphere, they turn to vapour and become visible as small lights in the sky — shooting stars — and properly known as meteoroids. Only when meteoroids have landed on the surface of the Earth are they known as meteorites.

There are three main kind of meteorite that we are likely to find: iron meteorite consisting chiefly of iron-nickel alloys; stony-iron meteorite containing nickel-iron with some silicate materials; stony meteorite that are composed of silicates, notably olivine and pyroxene, with some plagioclase and a little nickel-iron.

Tektites are small glassy objects concentrated in certain parts of the world where they have taken on local names. Those from Bohemia and Moravia are called *moldavites*; those from southern Australia are *australites*; those from the south-east USA are *bediasites*; from Georgia *tektites*; and from the Philippines, *philippinites*, etc. At one time, tektites were thought to be meteorites but scientists now think they were formed by meteorite impacts on Earth, generating great heat, which melts existing rock.

Moldavite is probably the rarest with its translucent glassy appearance. Some specimens are so clear that they can be mistaken for coloured glass because they have no crystal shape at all. Most take the form of flattened teardrops, rounded pebbles, or irregular splinters, which does nothing to diminish its value because it is highly prized for its rarity and for the unique green colour that is its most distinctive characteristic.

The possibility remains that tektites really did come to Earth on meteorites, or on the tails of comets, and textbooks are always careful to emphasise that the real origin of moldavite is not known with any certainty. Medicinally there is no known usage although magically this cosmic 'debris' can be used in astral working.

## Pearl

Pearls are classically white or pink, but may also appear in delicate shades of black, blue, brown, cream, green, grey, violet or yellow. The finest specimens display a distinctive rainbow-like bloom, which is also known as 'orient of pearl'. The name derives from the Latin *perna,* meaning 'sea mussel'. They are formed by oysters and mussels as a response to irritation caused by the presence of foreign bodies within the shells.

Medicinally, pearls have been prescribed for all manner of ailments and were used in potions in India to increase stamina and virility; in China, the elixir was taken to renew youth and vigour. Magically, the pearl is linked to the Moon and Elemental Water. It boosts psychic energy levels, aids scrying and enables the wearer to make contact with spirits of springs, streams and pools. Pearls are use in magic for their attributes of increasing wisdom.

## Petrified wood

From the Greek root *petro* meaning 'rock' or 'stone', it literally means 'wood turned into stone' and is the name given to a special type of fossilized remains of terrestrial vegetation. It is the result of a tree having turned completely into stone by the process of permineralization. All the organic materials have been replaced with minerals (mostly a silicate, such as quartz), while retaining the original structure of the wood.

Unlike other types of fossils which are typically impressions or compressions, petrified wood is a three dimensional representation of the original organic material. The petrifaction process occurs underground, when wood becomes buried under sediment and is initially preserved due to a lack of oxygen, which inhibits aerobic decomposition. Mineral-laden water flowing through the sediment deposits minerals in the plant's cells and as the plant decays, a stone mould forms in its place.

In general, wood takes less than 100 years to petrify, although the organic matter needs to become petrified before it decomposes completely

Medicinally, petrified wood has no known uses, but magically it is known as a stone of knowledge, a guide for contacting the Ancestors and for learning about the ancestral past, ancient ways, and wisdom of the Ancestors.

Many of these natural 'gems' can be obtained for very little cost and because they have their own special link to the past, their magical uses can be extremely useful, if not powerful aids in spell-casting.

## Try this exercise

### Animal, vegetable or mineral: Natural amulets

Natural talismans or amulets take many forms. In additional to precious gemstones, minerals and metals, items such as herbs, or the teeth and claws of animals, were used to fulfil the same purpose. Some were moulded into the image of the supernatural power they were supposed to represent.

- Make your own animal (fauna) amulet by obtaining a piece of horn or ivory and use it to harness the power of vitality and virility on both a physical or mental level. The horn or ivory may be carried in the form of a key ring, or piece of personal jewellery.

- Petrified wood or jet represents the vegetable (flora) world and harnesses its powers of protection and enlightenment. Carry in a pouch to avoid being handled by other people.

- The power of the mineral world can be harnessed by using tektites or fossils in amulet form for piercing the veil between worlds, and increasing conscious contact between the higher and lower Self. Keep hidden in a pouch and avoid interference from outside negativity.

Because these are natural gems, they will all react differently for different people. Don't be afraid to experiment and see which amulet works best for you.

# Chapter Nine

# Variations on an Original Theme

*"The truth of nature,"* wrote the philosopher Democritus, *"lies in deep mines and caves. The stability of what is seen and felt beneath our feet is an illusion ... below the surface, there are cracks and fissures and pockets of stale, trapped air; stalagmites and helactites, and unmapped dark rivers that flow ever downward. It is a place of caverns and stone waterfalls, a labyrinth of crystal tumours and frozen columns where history becomes future, and then becomes now."*

The magical nature of crystals, however, is still closely affiliated to belief in the recognition of supernatural agencies in control of the forces of Nature; and inextricably linked to science — although it *is* necessary to be able to differentiate between 'logical premise', and the symbolism based upon 'imagined powers and correspondences' in Nature. Simply because wishful thinking is the enemy of successful magical practice — and we must be able to experiment freely and not have our judgement clouded by superstition or dogma.

In reality, the magical applications of ancient Egypt derived from the official State religion, and, together with the influences from Mesopotamia, permeated the magical systems of Asia Minor and Syria, only to reappear in later Hebrew and Hellenic culture. The Graeco-Romano influences blossomed into Gnosticism, and subsequent esoteric practices of Eastern astrology, coupled with a neo-Platonic concept of the universe combined to develop the system of Hermetic/Qabalistic philosophy, which was to exert a lasting influence on Western ritual magic up to the present day.

The Old Italian (Etruscan) culture was highly sympathetic to superstition and esoteric belief, and although Imperial Rome itself contributed little to the development of ritualised magic, it was obsessed with the rites of divination and augury. As Joan Evans remarks in *Magical Jewels*, the persecution of magical practitioners under Augustan law "gave it the seal of degradation, and the Christian condemnation of all pagan rites as 'magical' added to the confusion of its definition."

Nevertheless, the belief in magic and divination had become too much a part of the people's heritage to be stamped out by Papal condemnation. While the early Church, wittingly or unwittingly, drew this heritage into its own symbolism, it also absorbed "a body of practice that had become Christian and was almost unconsciously magical: miraculous relics, charms and amulets invoking the aid of the Trinity, the Virgin, the Saints, and all the hierarchy of Heaven." The church opposed magic in all its forms, and condemned the engraved talisman, although it enthusiastically maintained the tradition of the *medicinal* amulet and holy relic.

**Remember: Fact has nothing to do with belief; *that the ancients believed*, is all we need to know. And even if we think we are no longer susceptible to the powers of the Old Gods, we only have to look through the eyes of an ancient Egyptian, Greek, Roman, Celt or Viking to see them.**

So, some may ask, why can't we just abandon the use of these ancient symbols? The experienced magical practitioner understands that contact with these 'old energies' can be attained more completely through symbols that are so ancient that they are buried deep within the storehouse of our collective subconsciousness. According to ritual magician and author, Kenneth Grant, the alternatives — intellectual formulae and symbols of mathematics and science — have been evolved too recently to serve as direct conduits. The magician or mystic uses the more direct paths, which long ago were mapped out in the shadowlands of what psychologist, Carl Jung referred to as the racial or universal unconscious.

## Names or Words of Power

Interestingly, Joan Evans goes on to point out that one of the most important types of medieval magical jewel is rarely mentioned in the lapidaries, and does not derive its power from the virtue of any gem. Names and 'words of power' are found in early magical texts, and the author of the treatise on the *Mysteries of the Egyptians* (usually ascribed to Iamblichus), asserts that such names of Mesopotamian and Egyptian origin have peculiar virtues, and are particularly to be venerated on account of their antiquity.

As Western ritual and ceremonial magic progressed, it took on a language of its own (see Chapter Five), using Hebrew and Gnostic traditions of not writing the name of god but introducing the use of numerology, often incomprehensible symbolism, coupled with purposely obscure inscriptions. Nevertheless, the magical use of names is rooted in many civilised people's minds today, just as it was in ancient and primitive societies; often a man's real name being kept secret because if it became known to a hostile magician, he could gain power over the man and destroy him. Professor Elizabeth M. Butler writing in *Ritual Magic*, states:

> "The ineffable names of the Qabalah were used and misused by the magical confraternity quite as profusely as those of the divinities of Egypt, Greece and Christendom. The holier the names, the more powerful they were supposed to be; and even the divine appellations of the Qabalistic sephiroth did not escape magical pollution."

What Professor Butler, along with thousands of others who read and write about magical practice, fails to grasp is that the 'magical' usage comes from the *way* the Names of Power are utilised, not from the name itself. As we have already discussed, this effectiveness is also dependent upon the hour, day or month when the work was carried out; the influence of planets, stars or constellations that were in the ascendant at the time were also believe to infuse a subtle essence into the stone as the sigil or image was being engraved.

The belief in the magical properties of stones and gems is of deepest antiquity, and the attribution of magical or mystical force to words and letters naturally led to the development of these inexplicable magical inscriptions. But as Joan Evans observes, rarity, strangeness and beauty have in them an inexplicable element, and the inexplicable is always potentially magical.

## Sympathetic Magic

A great deal of magical working is based upon what we call 'sympathetic magic', and for all the contemporary writing on the subject, sometimes older texts often convey the simplest interpretation, even if there was little actual belief or understanding. For example, Sir James Frazer's *Golden Bough* defines the subtle differences in magical practice as sympathetic magic (or the Law of Sympathy) being divided into two separate approaches – homoeopathic or imitative magic (the Law of Similarity) and contagious or contact magic (the Law of Contact).

Both work on the principle of events being controlled from a distance by utilising an item to represent the recipient, or by arranging to place an item in close proximity to the target. Both types of sympathetic magic can be used to cure or curse, but as we've seen in earlier chapters, magical workings (i.e. amulets and talismans), the images (or Names/Words of Power) engraved on the stones were believed to have a greater or lesser degree of effectiveness, independent of the properties contained with the gemstones themselves. So, to generate the maximum magical power, the virtue of the image *must* be of the same association as the virtue inherent in the stone — the amulet being less powerful when this was not the case.

Unfortunately, much of Frazer's writing is concerned with folklore from around the globe, rather than recording actual magical practices, but he does manage to categorise magical application in a way that would probably never occur to a real practitioner. Purely for teaching purposes, we will utilise Frazer's magical division, bearing in mind that it was Aleister Crowley who said that magic was a blend of art and science.

The general heading of magical practice often falls into two completely separate categories. The first is the theoretical (or pseudo-science) so beloved by armchair magicians who study a lot and write books, but who rarely put theory into practice. The second category is practical magic, which is also divided into two branches — the positive and the negative.

And when we talk about positive and negative magic, this is not a reference to 'black' or 'white' magical practice, since if we study the old texts in depth, we find that none of them use crystals and stones to attract negative/dark energy. Positive magic says: 'Do this in order that so and so may happen' while negative magic says: 'Do not do this, lest so and so may happen'. The aim of positive magic is to produce a desired event; the aim of negative magic is to avoid an undesirable one. Both consequences, however, of the desirable and the undesirable, can be brought about by the use of crystals and stones in accordance with Frazer's laws of similarity and contact.

A simple explanation ... but nevertheless an effective one.

## Divination by Stones and Crystals

Divination is the predicting of future events, or the discovery of "secret matters by a great variety of means, signs and occult techniques" according to *Traditional Witchcraft for Urban Living*, but before we can perform this successfully, we need to develop the art of 'seeing'. It is important to realise that whatever method is used for divination, those results are not cast in stone!

Divination reveals the future as relating to the past and the present, and what will happen if the warnings are not heeded in order to change things *before* they go wrong. The answer is also subjective to where an individual is standing at the precise moment in time at which they pose the question.

It is also a long-known fact that a hypnotic state can be induced by gazing fixedly on a bright object held just above the eyes; but from a seer's perspective a similar (though not so pronounced effect) results from gazing into or at, a bright object just before the seer's eyes. George Frederick Kunz explains that in the case of coloured gemstones, the effects of the various colour-rays combine with the light effects and strengthen the impression upon the optic nerve. There are, however, various different methods of divination using stones and crystals, for example:

**Crystallomancy** — an ancient practice of casting lots using small stones or crystals. Unlike crystalomancy, by which images or messages are received by meditating in a crystal ball, the results depend on the placement of the stones. Interpretation is accomplished through images or correspondences. This method requires specific crystals (or stones) being cast onto a circle, marked out with divisions for the past present and future. The 'lots' are deciphered according to the influence of the stone and its placement within the circles. It is this system that *Magic Crystals, Sacred Stones* is developing within the exercises following each chapter.

**Lithomancy** — divination by tossing coloured stones, particularly crystals or gems to foretell the future or interpret omens. May also refer to scrying with jewels and crystals, and which is considered to be one of the oldest forms of divination — that is, studying the gem or crystal and interpreting the visions or vibrations generated by the stone. Here a specific gem is placed in a quite area, and a light source is reflected off the natural sides or cut facets of the stone. Through studying and interpreting the play of light, the visions seen in the gem, or messages received telepathically will answer the querent's question. According to *Book of Divining the Future*, natural crystals and gemstones were used for this purpose by most ancient civilisation, including the Aztecs, the Incas, the Babylonians and the Egyptians.

In addition to their use in scrying, crystals can still be used for meditation and heightening intuition. Specific crystals are alleged to have specific divinational or helping qualities: i.e. if a person carries a certain crystal, they will be assisted by that crystal's power: "For example, to increase psychic ability, it is suggested that a diamond or peridot be worn or carried. A bronze or sapphire crystal will help in channelling. And a Herkimer diamond or fire opal should be worn of carried to enhance clairaudience … To energise the crystal or gem one should leave it outdoors on a night with a full moon."

**Rune stones** — a divinationary tool used by the German and Nordic peoples, which were widespread in Europe by 100 AD. In the early 1990s, European mystics and occultists became increasingly interested in the runes (from the German word *raunen*, meaning 'a secret' or 'mystery') and runic bronze rings were given to soldiers in WWI to protect them in battle. Most sets of runes contain 25 stones and in the traditional versions, all the stones are marked with historical symbols — except one, which is blank — and derived from the pictographic language of the early Norse. A set of runes can be made by selecting small stones with flat sides, such as those found at the beach or at a river's edge, and marking them with the appropriate symbols or letters.

**Crystalomancy** — divination by studying a crystal ball. There is evidence of the use of crystal balls as a means of divination in medieval times, and this form of scrying produces the most satisfactory results. The points of light reflected from the ball's polished surface serves to attract the attention of the gazer and then to fix the eye, until gradually the optic nerve becomes so fatigued that it finally ceases to transmit to the sensorium the impression made from without, and begins to respond to the reflex action proceeding from the brain of the gazer. In this way, the impression received from within is apparently projected and seems to come from without.

It is easy to understand that the results must vary according to the idiosyncrasy of the various scryers, for everything depends upon the sensitiveness of the optic nerve. In many cases the effect of prolonged gazing upon the brilliant surface will simply produce a loss of sight, the optic nerve will be temporarily paralysed, and may not respond to stimulation from within or without. In other cases the nerve will only be deadened, while retaining sufficient activity to react against a stimulus from the brain centres. It is almost invariably stated that, prior to the appearance of the desired visions, the crystal seems to disappear and a mist rises before the gazer's eyes. (George Frederick Kunz, *The Curious Lore of Precious Stones*). It was at Mortlake, on 22$^{nd}$ December 1581, that Dr John Dee made his first experiment with his crystal ball, which began with a pious invocation to the angel of the stone. Although Dee probably used more than one crystal in the course of his experiments, the most famous is the cairngorm, or smoky-quartz crystal, now on exhibition at the British Museum.

One method of scrying using the crystal ball is to place the crystal on a table and protect it from the reflections of surrounding objects by means of a velvet screen. Seven candle-sticks should be placed in front of the screen. The candles are then to be lit, the room being otherwise in complete darkness. The scryer should seat themselves with the hands laying flat upon the table either side of the crystal. Gaze fixedly into the crystal for half an hour or longer and the light from the candles will certainly ensure a multitude of light points in the crystal.

Beginners are advised to limit the duration of the experiment at first to five minutes, during which they should think of nothing in particular while keeping the eyes fixed intently upon the ball. Sometimes the image is distinctly perceptible on or about the surface of the crystal, while at other times the visual perception will be rather indefinite and clouded, although accompanied by strong mental impressions. The image *thought* to be seen on, before, or behind the crystal is in its essence a fancied projection on a purely mental image conceived in the brain. Nevertheless, the 'message' conveyed by the image is the answer to the seeker's question.

**Obsidian mirror:** Obsidian is a beautiful form of natural glass that is found in areas of volcanic activity and has been known since prehistoric times when it was widely used in weaponry and grave goods. Although it is a gemstone, it does not have a distinct chemical composition and is therefore classed as a rock formation. Dr John Dee, advisor to Queen Elizabeth I also used a black mirror of obsidian as a 'shew stone' and this, along with other of his metaphysical objects and tools are now in the British Museum.

Mirror magic can be applied in many forms. In one form or another it has been practised down through the ages and, particularly in England, persisted right up until the latter half of the 19th century in most rural areas. The basic principles of mirror magic can be clearly recognised in surviving folklore and rural superstitions. The Aztecs in particular, however, set great store by the powers of obsidian; it was known as Iztli or Teotetl, which means 'divine stone'. Artefacts have included images of the gods and sacrificial knives were made from obsidian. They also polished it and made it into special scrying mirrors, sacred to the god Tezcatlipoca, whose name means 'shining mirror', and who had one of his feet replaced with a round obsidian mirror

Obsidian mirrors can be used for scrying, divination, regressive viewing, looking at the present, or into the future; used to help find hidden or lost objects, but also to help seek out a hidden enemy by showing a face or image that give an idea of the person involved. In some cases, they can be used to spy on (or over-look) people, if the reason is justified. Magical practitioners use a mirror to deflect any possible negative energy that may be coming in their direction, and place them strategically around the house to help deflect psychic attack

**Method:** Place the obsidian mirror against a black ground about 3–4 feet away from you, preferably at face level, with a nightlight or small candle below your face, which gives the impression of a floating, reflective mask. Concentrate on your mirrored image and try not to blink. Allow your face to slide out of focus and, with practice, this is when impressions should begin to appear.

Remember, however, to close down the mirror correctly, either by passing your hands backwards and forwards in front of the glass, or by making the sign of the banishing pentagram between you and the mirror. Always keep the mirror covered with a piece of silk when not in use … and do not let anyone else look into it.

## Obsidian

Some obsidian contains small white crystals that make the surface of the stone resemble a snowstorm. Snowflake obsidian is the rarest and most valuable form of obsidian, which is basically an extrusive igneous rock composed of natural glass

## Try this exercise:

The exercises given at the end of each chapter in this book are designed for the purpose of creating your own personal system of divination by crystallomancy, the ancient practice of casting lots using small stones or crystals. The next step is to create a linen cloth for divinational purposes — using three circles to represent the past, present and future.

- Take a large white linen napkin and in the centre draw a circle the size of a large dinner plate; now place a tea plate in the centre of the first circle and draw a second circle; finally take a teacup or mug and draw a third circle inside the second circle. The centre circle represents Past, the inner circle the Present and the outer circle the Future.

- Now select 12 small pebbles from your collection. Remember that each stone has been discovered under unusual circumstances, or is one that you just felt the need to pick up and possess. Whatever the reason for your selection, these small stones are 'special', so you will recall exactly where and under what circumstances you found them — what their significance has for you, and how they will influence your 'reading'.

- Holding the 12 stones cupped between the palms of your hands, drop them onto the cloth and observe how they scatter. Disregard any that fall outside the outer circle. Those in the centre circle will refer to the past, which may have a bearing on the present and the future. The stones in the middle circle refer to the here and now; those in the outer circle are linked to the future.

- Now begin your first reading by identifying what each stone means to you, i.e. good or bad news. Remember, the 'lots' are deciphered according to the influence of the stones and their placement within the circles — revealing the future as relating to the past and the present, and what will happen if the warnings are not heeded in order to change things *before* they go wrong.

The most remarkable thing about divination is its overwhelming success — but before setting yourself up as a 'seer' for other people, you will need to create a separate set of stones from those used for your own personal readings to avoid unwanted psychic transference. Remember that the future is not fixed, and any advanced warning enables us to make the necessary changes to our lives before anything takes a turn for the worse.

## Chapter Ten

# Sacred Song of Reconciliation

As rare and costly as many of them are, beautiful or unusual stones were supposed to possess mystic and occult powers. Some were thought to be the abode of spirits, sometimes benevolent and sometimes malevolent, but always endowed with the colour to influence human destinies for good or ill. One of the earliest texts listing the symbolical significance of the colours of gemstones — and one of considerable length — was the *Della storia naturale delle Gemme* (1730) by Giacinto Gimma, who had gathered together a great quantity of material on the subject. For example:

- **Yellow stones** worn by a man stood for secrecy or discretion; when worn by a woman generosity. Golden yellow symbolised the Sun and the stone was chrysolite of the yellow jacinth; the animal correspondence was the lion, no doubt from the association of the zodiacal sign of Leo with the mid-summer sun. Garments of this colour were a sign of grandeur and nobility. Of the seven ages of man, yellow signified adolescence.

- **White stones** signified friendship, religion and integrity for men; for women contemplation, affability and purity. The colour, associated with the moon and Monday, was represented by a pearl; the animal correspondence was ermine (the winter colour of the stoat). The mystic number was seven, and white was the colour of infancy.

- **Red stones** symbolised for a man command, nobility,

lordship and vengeance; for a woman, pride, obstinacy and haughtiness. This was the colour of Mars and of Tuesday, and represented by a ruby and a lynx. It indicated full manhood and its number was the potent nine, three multiplied by itself. Occult books were often bound in red leather.

- **Blue stones** stood for wisdom and high, imaginative thought in a man; for a woman, jealousy in love, politeness and vigilance. It represented Venus and Friday; and was considered the symbol of childhood. The magical number was six; the animal correspondence was the goat; and the contemplation of the heavens and of the heavenly bodies. The study of stellar influences were all typified by the 'celestial-blue sapphire'.

- **Green stones** signified in men, joyousness, transitory hope and the decline of friendship; for women it meant unfounded ambition, childish delight and change. Mercury and Wednesday were attributed to green, together with the wily fox. The typical green stone was the emerald — youth is the age of man represented by the colour green, and five the magic number expressing it.

- **Black stones** signified gravity, good sense, constancy and fortitude; for young women, fickleness and foolishness, but for mature women, constant love and perseverance. The planet Saturn and Saturday were denoted by black, but the diamond was selected to represent this sombre hue, together with the boar and the number eight. Black was also the colour of envy; legal books were often bound in black leather.

- **Violet stones** represented sober judgement, industry and gravity in a man; in a woman, high thoughts and religious love. It was the colour of the planet Jupiter and of Thursday; the corresponding animal was the bull. Violet was the colour of old age and associated with the number three.

For a completely different magical viewpoint there are also the correspondences assigned by ritual magicians for the use of precious stones ...

## The Magical Correspondences of *Liber 777*

It was Aleister Crowley who took the age-old beliefs in the powers (or correspondences) of the sacred stones and formulated them into a workable system of Western ritual magic based on the Qabalah, and published his results in *Liber 777 and Other Qabalistic Writings*. Note, however, that there are only a few instances where these gems correspond to the traditional listings of birth/zodiacal stones.

Here we have the 'Heavens of Assiah' with the Planets following the Sephiroth of the Tree of Life. Numbers 1–10 correspond to the ten Sephiroth and numbers 11–32 correspond to the paths that join the Sephiroth. According to Crowley, numbers 31 and 32 must be supplemented by 31–bis and 32–bis two paths possessing a double attribution: 31–bis to Spirit against 31 to Fire; 32–bis to Earth as against 32 to Saturn — with the corresponding precious stones assigned to each level.

1. Sphere of Primum Mobile — Diamond
2. Sphere of the Zodiac or Fixed Stars — Star Ruby or Turquoise
3. Sphere of Saturn — Star Sapphire or Pearl
4. Sphere of Jupiter — Amethyst and Sapphire
5. Sphere of Mars — Ruby

| | | |
|---|---|---|
| 6. | Sphere of Sol | Topaz or Yellow Diamond |
| 7. | Sphere of Venus | Emerald |
| 8. | Sphere of Mercury | Opal, especially Fire Opal |
| 9. | Sphere of Luna | Quartz |
| 10. | Sphere of the Elements | Rock Crystal |
| 11. | Elemental Air | Topaz or Chalcedony |
| 12. | Mercury | Opal or Agate |
| 13. | Luna | Moonstone, Pearl or Crystal |
| 14. | Venus | Emerald or Turquoise |
| 15. | Aries | Ruby |
| 16. | Taurus | Topaz |
| 17. | Gemini | Alexandrite, Tourmaline or Iceland Spar |
| 18. | Cancer | Amber |
| 19. | Leo | Cat's Eye |
| 20. | Virgo | Peridot |
| 21. | Jupiter | Amethyst or Lapis Lazuli |
| 22. | Libra | Emerald |
| 23. | Elemental Water | Beryl or Aquamarine |
| 24. | Scorpio | Snakestone |
| 25. | Sagittarius | Jacinth |
| 26. | Capricornus | Black Diamond |
| 27. | Mars | Ruby or any red stone |
| 28. | Aquarius | Artificial Glass or Chalcedony |
| 29. | Pisces | Pearl |
| 30. | Sol | Crysoleth |
| 31. | Elemental Fire | Fire Opal |

| 32. Saturn | Onyx |
|---|---|
| Elemental Earth 32 bis | Salt |
| Spirit 31 bis | ... |

In *Liber 777*, Crowley explains why each stone is assigned to the various stages of the Tree of Life, and why many of them have dual symbolism. In his own inimitable literary style he explains, "These attributions are somewhat bold. The Star Sapphire refers to Nuit and the Black Diamond to the idea of NOX — Zero. It is invisible yet contains light and structure in itself ... The Diamond is white brilliance; it is pure carbon, the foundation of all living structure ..."

Although Crowley believed that magic was the alchemical product of science and art, there was an extremely valid reason why he continued to use what might be viewed as these outdated symbols of sorcery and superstition. As we discussed earlier, the answer is that the occultist understands that contact with these energies may be established more completely through the use of these ancient symbols: "To such symbols the Forces respond swiftly and with incalculable fullness ..."

## Alchemy & the Philosopher's Stone

The famous term, 'the Philosopher's Stone' refers to the Great Work of the alchemist, which is to find or create the Stone that could transmute impure substance into a rarefied state. Alchemy is also an ancient 'science' and the forerunner of chemistry, despite its earlier view that the transformation of base metal into gold was similar to the perfection of the human soul on reaching heaven — and therefore possible. Not surprisingly, no alchemist would reveal their trade secrets and so they also created a confusing secret language and symbolic code, designed to mislead the uninitiated. Alchemical texts were not written to provide outsiders with information, and were frequently couched in this symbolic language "so deliberately obscure that it has largely defied interpretation ever since".

As Ponce de Leon observed in his *Quest for the Foundation of Youth,* whether the conscious aim of the alchemist was the discovery of an actual stone, or merely the discovery of some process for turning a valueless substance into one of great value, is not clearly ascertainable from the purposely vague and obscure treatise on alchemy …

Outsiders (or the uninitiated) writing about esoteric subjects have always fallen into the trap of taking magical instructions literally, and why many of these texts read as 'cloud cuckoo land' theories. In fact, most references to alchemy describe it as 'a false science' based on the pretence that gold could be made from other basic metals, and is still referred to as nothing more than fraudulent.

As Hans Bierdermann observed in 'Alchemy: a secret language of the mind' (*Man, Myth & Magic*), however, these were misguided descriptions, which failed to take into account the modern advances in the study of the philosophical and psycho-logical side of the subject. According to him, alchemy was more art than science, and it's most important and most interesting aspect "was the spiritual transformation of the alchemist himself." For the mystical alchemist, the art involved both a chemical and spiritual process that transmuted the alchemist "from a state of leaden earthly impurity to one of golden spiritual perfection."

Kings and princes, all anxious to find ways of increasing their wealth, employed tame alchemists on a literal basis, in the belief that they really could turn base metal into gold. And this is the image that has dogged alchemy ever since, as George Kunz relates:

*"… alchemists believed that several other stones possessing 'magical' virtues could be produced. Among them the Angelic stone, which gave power to see the angels in dreams and visions;*

*and also the Mineral stone, a substance by means of which common flints could be transmuted into diamonds, rubies, sapphires, emeralds, etc. Possibly some alchemists were glassmakers and fused the quartz with various mineral salts into an imitation of the gems, therefore having the colours but not the hardness ore other properties."*

Twentieth century psychologists like C. G. Jung, however, began to pay serious attention to the symbolism of alchemy, suggesting that the symbols — the snakes, dragons, lions and wolves, the springs and fountains, trees, castles, etc. — were not deliberately chosen by 'mystery-mongerers' out to impress the gullible, but again corresponded to the 'ageless realities of the human mind', or the universal unconscious. Whatever the truth, the myth of the Philosopher's Stone is firmly imprinted in our culture.

## Talismans and Amulets — Part Two

As we have seen, the use of engraved gems as talismans was inherited by Europe from the East. The characteristic or properties of such a talisman is its sigil or device, and this is usually of sacred or symbolic character, often connected with some celestial body of which the astrological influence is thus inherited.

The belief in the virtue of rare stones passed into the magical lore of the Babylonians, which was only a 'stone's throw' from being given a place in their astrological cosmos. As Joan Evans observes, "Since to them all things were subject to the influence of sidereal powers, it was natural that in Babylon the fetish stone should become the magical talisman by association with such a supernatural power." In fact, the word 'talisman' is derived from the Arabic for the influence of the heavenly bodies upon the universe'.

The later attribution of mystical force to words and letters (or Name) by the Gnostics naturally led to the development of magical inscriptions and alphabets. For example: the formula Abracax derives from the Persian Supreme Being, and in Greek notation it stands for 365, hence Abracax was said to preside over the 365 virtues, one of which is supposed to prevail on each day of the year. Abracax stones were carried as talismans, having the name engraved on them, or the symbolic forms combining a fowl's head, a serpent's body and human limbs, and which has given the name to a whole class of engraved magical gems, like this Assyrian cylinder, dating from 7<sup>th</sup> century BC:

*May the executor of this seal*
*be strong, be renewed,*
*be happy, and live to old age.*

Or a double-sided Greek inscription from the 6<sup>th</sup> century

*Lord, succour the wearer.*

According to Joan Evans (*Magical Jewels*) in medieval lapidaries of engraved gems of Italy, France and England astrological elements are certainly present, but a belief in the *magical* properties of engraved gems is not to be found either in Anglo-Saxon England, or Carolingian France, or in Western Europe before the Crusades. Its manifestation in Western Europe does not appear to be earlier than the latter half of the 12<sup>th</sup> century, having been brought in on the tide of ancient learning that was flowing in from Arabic Spain towards the southern coasts of France. In fact, the earliest references to magical engraved gems found in English documents occur in a collection of 12<sup>th</sup>-century manuscripts now in the Bodleian Library. Lapidaries of the Middle Ages, however, reveal how persistent was the belief in the magical virtues of gems, and the evidence of literature and the inventories of the period, proves that this belief was not merely theoretical but played a real part in everyday life.

## Phenomenal Gems

As we have already discussed — rarity, strangeness, and beauty have in them the inexplicable element, and the inexplicable is always potentially magical. And no gemstones have afforded more magical interest than those known as 'phenomenal gems', that is, those exhibiting phenomenal quality, either as a moving line (as in the chrysoberyl or quartz cat's eye), or as *asterism* (star-sapphire or star-ruby), or a moving light (moonstone). Then there is the alexandrite cat's eye effect, which, in addition to its chatoyant effect, changes from green to red, showing its natural colour by day, and glowing with a ruddy hue by artificial light.

The cat's eye effect is caused by a twinning of the crystal. When the gemstone is cut with a dome across the twinning line, this shows itself as a smooth band of white light, with a translucent or transparent space at one side; the line varying in sharpness and breath as the illumination becomes more intense. If the line is very bright, the line is no wider than the thinnest silver or platinum wire. The quartz cat's eye is less distinct than the chrysoberyl stone. When cut straight across, an apparent striation in the stone produces the cat's eye effect, but it is not as beautiful as the true cat's eye. The alexandrite variety is coloured by chromium and dichroitic, appearing green when viewed in one direction and red in another; in artificial light the green colour is lost and the red alone becomes apparent.

The moonstone with its silvery-white light changes on the surface as the light varies. This is due to chatoyancy produced by a reflection caused by certain cleavage planes present in feldspar of the variety to which the moonstone belongs.

Star Stones, or *asteria*, are the ultimate in rarity and magical significance, and although the most costly are the Star Sapphire and the Star Ruby, several other less precious varieties still produce this strange phenomenon, i.e. rose quartz spheres when held up to the light may reveal two bands of light intersecting to form a star. One of the most unique of talismanic stones, the star crystal is said to be so potent that it continues to exercise its influence over the first wearer, even when it has passed into other hands.

> *"The star sapphire, is a variety of sapphire in which, when the stone is cut and rounded off horizontal with the dome of the crystal, the light is condensed across the three lines of crystalline interference. Three cross lines produce a star that moves as a source of light, or as it is moved from the source of light. Star sapphires very rarely possess the familiar deep blue color of the fine blue sapphire; generally the color is somewhat impure, or of a milky-blue, or else a blue-gray, or sometimes almost a pure white. blue-gray, gray and white stones frequently show a much more distinct star possibly from the fact that there are more inclusions between the layers of the crystals than with the darker blue stones, as it is the set of interference bands that produce the peculiar light."*
>
> George Frederick Kunz, *The Curious Lore of Precious Stones*

Magically, the Star Sapphire refers to Nuit and "suggests the expanse of night with the Star appearing in the midst thereof ... The doctrine is that the stars are formed in the body of night by virtue of the form of that night by the impact of the energy of a higher plane" [(*Liber 777*) For the followers of Thelemic teaching, this is the most sacred of precious stones.

When the rutile inclusions inside the ruby form a geometric shape, they reflect light into a shiny six-pointed star, which gives the gem a distinctive sparkle. This beautiful and magical effect is also known as *asterism* and it happens quite by accident, since the inclusions can often create flaws in otherwise perfect gemstones. Magically, the Star Ruby represents the male energy of the Creator Star, and in his magical encyclopaedia, *The Equinox*, Aleister Crowley includes two rituals: The Star Ruby and The Star Sapphire.

Needless to say, the medieval alchemist searching for the

Philosopher's Stone, sailed uncomfortably close to heresy simply because he relied on his own efforts to confront God face to face, rather than approaching the Divine through the conventional medium of the Church. But even if we take alchemy and religion out of the equation, there are numerous parallels we can draw with the relatively new science of geology. In fact, it is the metallic elements acting as *impurities* in the gems that give most their colour.

According to Richard Cavendish writing in *The Magical Arts*, the attributes of the Philosopher's Stone were uncanny similar to the rocks and minerals that are the building blocks of the Earth's crust, and have been forming and reforming for billions of years.

> *"... it is something which exists everywhere in Nature, but is generally regarded as worthless. It is made of animal, vegetable and mineral; it has a body, a soul and a spirit; it grows from flesh and blood; it is made of fire and water. It is a stone, but it is not a stone, unknown yet known to everyone, despised and yet unimaginably precious; coming from God but not coming from God ..."* (The Magical Arts)

It is undeniable that many of our magic crystals and sacred stones can be found everywhere across the globe, but are generally considered worthless in the eyes of those who have no affinity with them. From the organic sedimentary rocks (which are composed mostly of the remains of once-living organisms) to the creation of the 'organic minerals' (that come from plants and animals), we have rocks that have metamorphosed from the pressures of fire and water. And if we subscribe to the belief that all natural things, both animate and inanimate, are imbued with a life force of their own, then even the rocks are part of the World Soul, or spirit.

By the same token, the priceless diamond in its natural state is unknown to most people, although everyone is familiar with the famous stones in the Crown Jewels — even if we despise the methods surrounding the mining of them. Lastly and depending on our personal belief, we may see the Earth as being a creation of God ... or as a result of the Big Bang. So, if we increase our knowledge of the way the Earth has shaped its bones over the billions of years since it was first formed out of cosmic gasses, we will come to a greater wisdom and understanding about our place in the Universe. And in taking the first steps on this new journey of discovery, we may find that, in Richard Cavendish's words, a humble piece of quartz can become our own personal Philosopher's Stone that leads from "a state of leaden earthly impurity to one of golden spiritual perfection."

## Try this exercise

### Make a personal talisman or amulet

As we have seen throughout this book, magic crystals and sacred stones have been widely used as talismans and amulets since the beginning of human history. These were objects supposedly endowed with supernatural or magical power — in particular the power to avert evil or misfortune. The difference between an amulet and a talisman as a magical tool lies in the preparation rather than the purpose.

- By now you will have found a very special stone, gem or crystal that has a very strong appeal for you. It doesn't need to be anything expensive — just something that has a very special significance.

- Hebrew amulets differed from those of the Christians, because Mosaic Law forbade the representation of human or animal form, and Jewish people were only permitted to wear or carry amulets engraved with characters of mystic or symbolic significance. This custom passed into Western ritual magic.

- To generate the maximum magical power, the virtue of the image *must* be of the same association as the virtue inherent in the stone — the amulet being less powerful when this is not the case.

- Originally, incantations and magic spells were chanted over them to invest them with magical powers, but later civilisations began to inscribe magical symbols onto the talisman or amulet.

- An amulet is kept with us at all times, often in the form of a piece of jewellery, key fob, pendant, or carried loose in a bag or pocket. It requires little or no special preparation and is intended to deflect trouble in a very general sense in other words a good luck charm.

- A talisman should only be carried for a limited period while the 'spell' is activated, and is aimed at a specific purpose or outcome. The exact nature of the talisman's protective power will be governed by the amount of effort and concentration that goes into the final preparation.

An amulet or lucky charm can be given away as a gesture of friendship, but a talisman, once it has served its purpose, should be disposed of by fire or running water. The spell or incantation will, of course, depend on the spiritual Tradition of the magical practitioner, and should be disposed of according to the teachings of that particular Path.

# Sources & Bibliography

*Alchemy*, Diana Fernando (Blandford)

*Ancient Energies of the Earth*, David Cowan and Anne Silk (Thorsons)

*Britain BC*, Francis Pryor (Harper Collins)

*Calendars & Constellations*, Emmeline Plunket (Senate)

*Chinese Gods: The Unseen World of Spirits & Demons*, Keith Stevens (Collins & Brown)

*Concise Encyclopaedia of Heraldry*, Guy Cadogan Rothery (Bracken)

*The Curious Lore of Precious Stones*, George Frederick Kunz (Dover)

*Earth Mysteries*, Philip Heselton (Element)

*The Equinox*, Aleister Crowley (Falcon)

*A Field Guide to Rocks & Minerals*, Frederick H. Pough (Constable)

*Gems From The Equinox*, Aleister Crowley (Weiser)

*The Gemstones Handbook*, Christine Sempers (Raven)

*Geology*, I. O. Evans (Warne)

*Geology & Scenery in England & Wales*, A. E. Trueman (Pelican)

*The Goat-Foot God*, Dion Fortune (Aquarian)

*History of Art*, H. W. Janson (Reprint Society)

*The Hollow Tree*, Mélusine Draco (ignotus)

*How To Make Amulets, Charms & Talismans*, Deborah Lippman and Paul Colin (Cassell)

*Illustrated Encyclopaedia of Minerals*, ed. Dr Alan Woolley (Gallery)

*Journeys From the Centre of the Earth*, Iain Stewart (Century)

*Liber 777*, Aleister Crowley (Weiser)

*The Making of the English Landscape*, W. G. Hoskins (Pelican)

*The Magical Arts*, Richard Cavendish (Arkana)

*Magical Jewels*, Joan Evans (Dover)

*Mineral & Rocks*, Keith Lye (Rainbow)

*Needles of Stone*, Tom Graves (Gothic Image)

*Pebble Polishing*, Edward Fletcher (Blandford)

*The Penguin Dictionary of Geology,* D. G. A. Whitten with .J R. V.
  Brooks (Penguin)
*The Phenomenology of Landscape,* Christopher Tilley (Berg)
*Pocket Guide to Minerals,* Andrew Clark (Gallery)
*Priestess,* Alan Richardson (Aquarian)
*Qabalistic Writings of Aleister Crowley* (Weiser)
*Riches of the Earth,* Frank J. Anderson (Windward)
*Ritual Magic,* Elizabeth M. Butler (Sutton)
*Rocks & Minerals,* E. P. Bottley (Octopus)
*The Secret Country,* Janet and Colin Bord (BCA)
*A Study of History,* Arnold Toynbee (BCA)
*Talisman, Charms & Amulets,* Robert W. Wood (Rosewood)
*Traditional Witchcraft for the Seashore,* Melusine Draco (O-Books)
*Traditional Witchcraft for Urban Living,* Melusine Draco (O-Books)
*Treasures of the Earth,* ed by Chris Pellant (Orbis)
*Spells, Charms, Talismans & Amulets,* Pamela A. Ball (Arcturus)
*What You Call Time,* Suzanne Ruthven (ignotus)

Axis Mundi Books provide the most revealing and coherent explorations and investigations of the world of hidden or forbidden knowledge. Take a fascinating journey into the realm of Esoteric Mysteries, Magic, Mysticism, Angels, Cosmology, Alchemy, Gnosticism, Theosophy, Kabbalah, Secret Societies and Religions, Symbolism, Quantum Theory, Apocalyptic Mythology, Holy Grail and Alternative Views of Mainstream Religion.